Reba craved attention. She called her brother Pake over and begged him to sing with her; she wanted in on the action too. Even at the age of five, she was not much of a spectator; she always wanted to be in the spotlight, the center of attention. Pake relented and the two sang "Jesus Loves Me." When they had finished, a cowboy gave her a nickel. That little event would always be something Reba would remember. Years later, she said, "That amazed me, people paying me to sing. I never forgot that."

REBA McENTIRE

COUNTRY MUSIC'S QUEEN

DON CUSIC

A 2M Communications Production

ST. MARTIN'S PAPERBACKS

REBA MCENTIRE: COUNTRY MUSIC'S QUEEN

Copyright © 1991 by Don Cusic.

Cover photograph by Retna.

Library of Congress Catalog Card Number: 91-20613

ISBN: 0-312-95342-9

Printed in the United States of America

St. Martin's Press edition published 1991
St. Martin's Paperbacks edition/ September 1994

10 9 8 7 6 5 4 3 2 1

This book is dedicated to my parents,

Lloyd and Mary Cusic.

CONTENTS

ACKNOWLEDGMENTS

I am indebted to a number of people for helping me while I was working on this manuscript.

At the Country Music Foundation in Nashville, I must thank Ronnie Pugh and others who work in the Archive—Becky Bell, John Rumble, Bob Pinson, Darlene Roger, Linda Gross, Charlie Seemans, and Chris Skinner—as well as the Executive Director, Bill Ivey, for their invaluable help.

At the Country Music Association, I appreciated the help of Kelley Gattis, Teresa George, and Helen Farmer.

At the Cowboy Hall of Fame in Oklahoma City, Don Reeves was an immense help, as was Judith Dearing of the Rodeo Historical Society, Marilyn Peil, Richard Rattenbury, and M. J. Van Deventer. The McAlester Historical Society's Joanne Cantrell and Nancy Ezell, as well as Alice Withrow at the Atoka Library, were also helpful.

Joe Carter at the Will Rogers Memorial in Claremore, Oklahoma, has been helpful in putting me up when I've wandered into his parts and has provided interesting conversations and lunches.

Steve Fleming and Sherry Compton, with the Professional Rodeo Cowboys' Association in Colorado Springs, provided some valuable information about John McEntire's rodeo days.

At the Center for Popular Music at Middle Tennessee State University in Murfreesboro, I appreciated the help of Ellen Garrison and Sarah Long. In the Department of Recording Industry Management at the same university, I must thank Geoff Hull and Dean Ed Kimbrell for their help and support.

I interviewed a number of people, asked others pertinent questions, and was able to chat with others to clarify various points during the time I was writing this book. These people included Clark Rhyne, Charlie Battles, Jenny Bohler, Ray Williams, Glenn Keener, Red Steagall, Lonnie Webb, Jerry Bailey, Joe Light, Robert Oermann, Tommy Goldsmith, Charles Wolfe, Liz Thiels, Jimmy Bowen, Larry Benson, and Bruce Hinton. I sincerely appreciate all of their help and input. I would also like to thank Cliff Gallespie.

I am especially indebted to my editor, Jim Fitzgerald, and my agent, Madeleine Morel, for all their help and support.

Finally, thanks to Delaney, Jesse, Eli, and Alex for taking my mind off this manuscript and getting me occupied in other activities so I don't spend all of my time writing and working.

It has been said the last shall be first and so it is with Jackie, whose help and support makes all this possible. Though she is last in these acknowledgments, she comes first in all the rest of my life.

PROLOGUE

From this valley they say you are going
We will miss your bright eyes and sweet smile

It's about six hundred miles from McAlester, Oklahoma, to Nashville, Tennessee. Reba Nell McEntire was born in McAlester on March 28, 1955. A few days after her birth, Clark and Jackie McEntire took their new baby girl—their third child and second daughter—home to their ranch in Chockie, just south of Kiowa.

When the baby looked out the window she could see horses and ranch land and people in cowboy hats working cattle. On TV the most popular shows were cowboy shows like "The Cisco Kid," "Wild Bill Hickok," "Annie Oakley," "Gene Autry," "Range Rider," and "Death Valley Days," as well as shows like "I Love Lucy," "You Bet Your Life," "Life of Riley," "Loretta Young," and "Dragnet."

The top-selling record in the country was "The Ballad of Davy Crockett," which came from the hit Disney series. In country music the number one record was "In the Jailhouse Now" by Webb Pierce. Top country stars on the charts that week were Faron Young, Red Foley, Eddie Arnold, Hank Snow, Carl Smith, Marty Robbins, Tennessee Ernie Ford, and Kitty Wells.

The McEntire house was usually filled with country songs from the radio and from Jackie's singing. Clark was a rodeo cowboy, like his daddy, roping steers all over the West and trying to take home some prize money. Some of little Reba's earliest memories are of hearing country music and seeing rodeos, traveling with her folks.

Chockie is about fifty miles north of the Red River, which separates Oklahoma and Texas. This area in southeastern Oklahoma is part of the Red River Valley, which ends around Chockie and Stringtown with the limestone hills that rise up from the land. This is where little Reba McEntire spent her young years, growing up on an Oklahoma ranch.

PART 1

GROWING UP

WITH THE RODEO

CHAPTER 1

The July moon hung like a fingernail in the western sky. Venus shone like a diamond further down the imaginary finger. It was 4 A.M. and Clark McEntire had been driving all night, heading to Cheyenne, Wyoming. His wife, Jacqueline, was dozing in the front seat; in the back, his four children were asleep. Susie and Reba were on the floorboard, Alice was on the seat, and Pake was stretched out on the ledge by the back windshield; all of them were lost in child dreams, oblivious to the miles rolling away beneath them.

The old green Ford hummed through the night toward Cheyenne, pulling a trailer with Clark's horse in it. Back home in Kiowa, Oklahoma, the cattle were out to pasture, fattening themselves with the summer grass. Out on the road, cowboys were traveling from rodeo to rodeo, competing for prize money, points for a championship, and bragging rights. Clark needed the rodeo money to help support his family and keep them going.

Clark was entered in the steer-roping event, and roping was on his mind. Two years earlier, in 1958, he had won the overall steer-roping championship saddle. That was the year he had won the same event in Cheyenne as well.

It must have been tough on the family, hitting the road to make all the rodeos, but they seemed to love it, and Clark liked having his family along. Not all the cowboys brought their families.

There are two kinds of rodeo cowboy. One kind rides in the wild-and-woolly events, like saddle bronc, bareback bronc, or bull riding. Those are mostly young guys—late teens and early twenties—because those events are a young man's game. To get on the back of a mean, mad, bucking Brahman bull, you've either got to have a tremendous amount of courage or just be plain fool enough to try. Sometimes it's hard to tell the difference between a brave man and a dang fool.

You don't need anything but the entry fee for these events. You show up, pays your money, and takes your chances. If you hang on for eight seconds and look good riding—look like you're in control and can rock back and forth with one arm high in the air, instead of hanging on for dear life with panicky desperation all over your face and your body jerked around like you're caught in a spastic, runaway machine that won't let you go—then you might win some money.

You also win the crowd. It's these bucking events that get the attention and glory. When you think of rodeos you think of some guy on a bucking bronc or bull. That's why the bull riding always comes last in a rodeo; it's what people want to see most—the scariest, dangerous, most exciting part of the whole rodeo. Even if a cowboy can stay on that bull's back long enough, he might get stomped or gored when he gets off. Broncs ain't nearly as mean, but their hooves can still cut you to pieces, and you can still break some bones when you hit the ground.

The other kind of rodeo cowboy is the one who goes for the timed, roping events. These guys tend to be a bit older, and they are generally working cowboys. Chances are the bronc and bull riders are really performers—they might not even live on a ranch. But the ropers live on ranches and actually work some head of cattle.

You've got to practice a lot to be good at roping. You've got to be smart and have a good horse too, because the horse is about seventy-five percent of roping. If you're going to do well roping, win some money, then you've got to bring your horse with you to the rodeos, and that means buying a trailer and feeding and caring for him. That's a lot more work than simply driving or flying from rodeo to rodeo so you can just climb on some cantankerous animal with a belt tight around his flanks to make him buck.

Clark McEntire had a ranch where he ran some head of cattle, and he wanted some more land, wanted to be a rancher. He may have sensed that one day his rodeo days would be over; there's always somebody younger and better coming along behind you. And the plain fact of the matter is that unless you are one of the handful of all-around top cowboys, you don't make a lot of money. Even when you make good money, you've got to keep up a horse and pay your traveling expenses and other upkeep. There's a big difference between "gross" and "net" in a cowboy's income. Somehow, the take-home pay doesn't always all get taken home.

CHAPTER 2

As the morning crept on, the sky began to lighten, turning from darkest black to muddy gray, then to a pale blue. The clouds on the eastern horizon became streaked with pink; further up in the sky they were purple. Soon the sky became a washed-out blue, and a slight haze could be seen hanging over the plains where the land rolled like waves on the ocean. The earth was starting to wake up.

Then the sun pushed up over the horizon, splashing light over the land, giving birth to a new day. A bright, fresh orange spotlight from the east, it shone with the energy of a child; the evening before it had looked like a tired old man going down with quiet dignity.

Soon the kids started waking up; they quickly grew restless, ready to get outside and run and play. But they couldn't do that inside a car rolling along the road. With four kids in such a small space, there'd be fights and fusses, crying and screaming and arguments that no parent could ever unravel: she hit him but he had called her a name but before that she had said something because yesterday he had done this or that but the reason he had done this or that was because . . . well, there was no use trying to find a reason behind it all.

Clark was a quiet man and not inclined to talk much, keeping his eyes on the road and just driving, driving, driving. Jackie would have to keep the kids orderly and entertained. There was no radio in the car, so she would get them to sing, doing funny songs like "Please Mr. Custer," "Wake Up, Little Susie," or "Does Your Chewing Gum Lose Its Flavor on the Bedpost Overnight," country songs, or maybe a gospel hymn like "How Great Thou Art."

That's how the McEntire kids learned harmony—singing in that car during those endless miles between rodeos. Sometimes they'd play games for a while or talk or try to play with a doll or something in their lap, but they always came back to singing.

Besides providing entertainment for the kids, the singing also helped keep their daddy awake and alert so he could make good time on that highway going from rodeo to rodeo. That's the nomadic life of a rodeo cowboy in the summer, covering those endless miles in the big, wide West. You're always trying to hit as many rodeos as you can on a weekend. Sometimes you don't make the qualifying times in one, so you scramble over to another; sometimes you have to decide where your best chance for winning is or where the biggest take-home pot is and go for that.

Jackie McEntire had always loved singing and was blessed with a beautiful voice, a voice some said was like Patsy Cline's. Jackie had wanted to try singing, but had been dissuaded by her parents, who were apprehensive about such a venture. Deeply religious, they considered entertaining for a living to be an open invitation to court sin and head towards Hell. So Jackie backed down and did not make a trip to California like she hoped; instead, she went to college and began teaching school. Then when she married Clark and had those four kids, there wasn't any time to even think about such a thing as a singing career. But she could pass on her love of singing to her kids, and that's what she did. And the child that seemed to have that love of singing more than the others had a beautiful voice too. That child was her third one, Reba Nell, and Jackie vowed to do all she could to help Reba in a singing career.

CHAPTER 3

They call it the "Daddy of 'Em All" or "The Big One," but the official name is "The Frontier Rodeo Days." It's held in Cheyenne, Wyoming, for nine days each July.

In 1960 the event had been extended to six days and, for the first time, included a show on Sunday. It was hot; the thermometer hit ninety. In spite of special events like the Air Force Academy band, a high-wire act, and Zachina being shot from a cannon over the top of the Ferris wheel, the event had the lowest attendance ever—only seven thousand people.

By the end of the event, the Republicans had nominated Richard Nixon for President; just before it began, the Democrats had nominated John Kennedy.

Out in the rodeo ring, Clark McEntire's rope came up a bit short; he lost the steer-roping contest to Don McLaughlin, who made enough money in the calf and steer roping to defend his title as all-around cowboy at Cheyenne.

In steer roping, the steer is released and the cowboy goes after it, spinning his rope above his head. He has to get that rope over the steer's horns—without getting penalized for having it go over the head and catching the steer by the throat—and then let the slack go down the steer's right flank. These are big animals, weighing five hundred to eight hundred pounds each. Once the rope is hooked over the horns, the cowboy pulls his horse to the left so the rope cuts the legs out from under the steer, knocking him down.

Unlike bull riding or bulldogging, the roping events evolved directly from the working life of a ranch cowboy. Steer roping seems to have gotten its start from cowboys having to rope and pull down a recalcitrant steer for one reason or another—maybe he kept wandering away from the herd and had to be convinced to stick with the rest of the bunch and not mosey off, or perhaps the old critter was sick and needed medicine, or maybe he just needed branding.

The event is not like calf roping, where a small calf is set loose and the cowboy must throw the rope over the head and jerk the calf down. You don't pick up a big steer and throw him down. That's the horse's job. After the steer is down, the horse has to keep the rope tight so the steer won't get up while the cowboy jumps off and gets his pigging string around three legs. As soon as he ties a "hooey"—the name of the knot—the cowboy throws up his arms and the timing judge puts down his flag to stop the clock. If the steer stays tied on the ground for six seconds it all counts.

In Cheyenne, Clark McEntire had to catch three steers after giving them a 30-foot lead. That was a little more fair for the cowboy than the first steer-roping contest at Cheyenne had been, when the roper had had to give the steer a 150-foot head start. That first winner in 1897 had averaged two minutes and thirty-five seconds for his roping. In 1958 Clark had averaged 22.2 seconds for each steer, and he had taken home top prize, a gold-plated belt buckle with five laurel rings across the middle, as well as the prize money. Cowboys treasure this Cheyenne belt buckle; it is more prized than any other.

But in 1960 the rope just didn't fall like it had in 1958 for Clark. It's a long drive back to Chockie from Cheyenne.

Back at the Frontier Hotel in Cheyenne, where the whole family of six stayed in one room, the cowboys gathered around in the lobby, laughing, joking, telling stories, and playing games. There was no TV in the room, so everybody hung around the lobby, creating their own entertainment. Everett Shaw, the legendary rodeo roper, was egging little Pake on, wanting him to sing. Pake did, performing "Hound Dog," and the cowboy gave him a quarter.

Little red-headed, freckle-faced Reba watched this. She was five years old, and it was tough being third in the family. Alice was oldest, with the privileges that came with that place; Pake was the only boy, so he got a lot of attention just for that. And Susie was the darling, the baby of the bunch.

Reba craved attention. She called Pake over and begged him to sing with her; she wanted in on the action too. Even at that age, Reba was not much of a spectator; she always wanted to be in the spotlight, the center of attention. Pake relented and the two sang "Jesus Loves Me." When they had finished, a cowboy gave her a nickel. That little event would always be something Reba would remember. Years later, she said, "That amazed me, people paying for me to sing. I never forgot that."

CHAPTER 4

In a small cemetery in Coalgate, Oklahoma, about thirty yards off the highway under a small cedar tree, is the grave of John McEntire. On his tombstone, beneath the dates of his birth and death, is carved the inscription "Lifetime Cowboy."

When you talk about cowboys and rodeos, the name John McEntire is liable to come up. Long before Reba McEntire was even a thought, the McEntire name was becoming well known in rodeo circles in the West. Indeed, John was probably the first "star" in the McEntire clan.

John Wesley McEntire was born in Lula, Indian Territory, on February 19, 1897. Lula—named for Lula Scott, the daughter of John Scott, an early resident—is in eastern Pontotoc County, southeast of Oklahoma City and northeast of Stonewall. He was the son of Clark and Helen McEntire, and his daddy was a story all his own.

Get this. If you think Reba McEntire is one-of-a-kind, it's just because she's following an old family tradition. It's been said about Pap McEntire that there never was another one like him on the planet Earth. That might be a gross understatement.

Clark Stephen "Pap" McEntire was born on a Mississippi riverboat on September 10, 1855. His father was a carpenter on riverboats, and the family had moved to Cairo, Illinois, after living in Virginia. The family had arrived in Norfolk in 1803. Before that, the McEntires (sometimes spelled McIntire or McIntyre) had come from Scotland, where the family had been boat builders. A large mallet the Scottish McEntires used in building boats has been handed down in the family, though no one is quite sure where it is today.

Later, the McEntires moved to Texas, and Pap's father, Reba's great-great-grandfather, is buried in Farmersville, Texas, northeast of Dallas and about twenty miles from the Oklahoma line.

Pap had married Alice Buié, from Bowie, Texas, and moved up to Indian Territory. They had two daughters, but within a six- or eight-month period Alice and the two girls died from a fever; they are buried near Ardmore, Oklahoma. Next Pap married an Indian woman, but that didn't work out, and then he married Helen Brown, from Archer City, Texas.

Pap and Helen had ten kids, of whom John, Reba's grandfather, was "about the third or fourth." Pap was a small man, but Helen was a big woman, and "they never did get along—fought all the time." In his later years Pap had a small, two-wheeled buggy that was only big enough for one person, so he carried his girlfriend around with one arm wrapped around her so she wouldn't fall out. That made Helen mad, understandably, "and she would get to thumpin' on him." Actually, Pap had several girlfriends "about like he was" and that "just about fit him."

Pap talked a lot about the Civil War; he would have been a young boy about five or so when William Quantrill was making his raids in Missouri. He certainly must have heard some firsthand stories from Civil War survivors.

He wore a rope necktie—made out of a real rope—every day of his life. One end of the rope was tied up tight around his neck and the other end hung down around his knees. He swore he never took a bath in his whole life. He never bought any clothes, either—just wore whatever he picked up. If somebody else was wearing a coat and laid it down, well, Pap picked it up and wore it until he took it off again. He always wore a rubber boot on one foot and a shoe on the other. According to Ray Williams, who lived with him as an adopted son, "his ankles looked like rusted pipes."

According to some who knew him, he got so hard to live with that he moved out to a chicken house on his farm. (Actually, he'd lost his place during the Great Depression to the Federal

11

Land Bank.) The chickens would roost on his headboard. When a chicken gets tired and sleepy it's easy to move, so before he went to bed, Pap would turn the chickens around so their droppings would not fall in his face.

The stove in the old chicken house was "a big pile of stones" and the coffee pot "was the blackest you ever saw." There was a stovepipe "held up with wire—it was the awfulest mess you ever saw." The door hinges were made from the rubber of an old tire that had been cut up, and Pap slept in a small, three-quarter bed he'd gotten out of some bunkhouse. He called this place his "Dutch oven."

There were always animals around—ten or fifteen dogs always followed him—and chickens were all over the place, along with guineas, goats, hogs, mules, horses, and cattle. Ray Williams often stayed with him out in the old chicken house and remembers that first thing every morning Pap would make him run the goats off before he got up.

The dogs caused a bit of a problem. They had the mange, and Pap caught it. Ray Williams remembers that Pap got him to swab motor oil all over Pap's body once to get rid of it. Pap always smelled a powerful heap.

He "stayed tanked up all the time" too, a result of imbibing healthy amounts of the mash beer made in the stills he hung around. He kept on hand a number of old jugs with corncob stoppers, and bees would buzz around them.

He apparently knew a number of outlaws and would take them in and hide them on his place. Some of the kids remember carrying a plate of food out to the barn to feed an outlaw or two. In fact, people remember one of Pretty Boy Floyd's partners staying on Pap's farm just a few days before the outlaw was killed.

Pap loved race horses and kept about twenty or thirty mares around. Ray remembers that Helen would get the kids to help Pap pack up and get away from the place when it was time to go to some races, "and then she'd pray he'd never come back.

But he always did." Pap and Helen fought "nearly every day of their life."

Pap was a farmer and raised a number of hogs. Ray remembers "those hogs were all over the place, and some of us kids were always having to go over to somebody's place to get the hogs out of their fields." Same with his other animals. He also raised mules and was "always breakin' a mule" on his farm.

Every Saturday Pap drove an old 1917 Model T truck with solid rubber tires to Coalgate about ten miles away. He seldom went over ten miles an hour, and kids used to jump on the back of his truck as he headed into town. When he got to town, he'd tell the load of kids—there was always a pretty good number hanging on his truck—what time he'd be leaving so they could hang on for the return trip. As he drove back, they'd drop off when they got near their own homes.

Later he got a Model T roadster he named "Hoopie." Pap thought the roadster might be rusting out, so one day he had Tod Rhyne take a mop and cover the Model T with old, dirty motor oil. So many chicken feathers got stuck to that roadster after that, it's a wonder it didn't take off and fly.

Pap's chicken house caught fire once, and one wall burned down. But Pap propped the wall back up as best he could and kept on living there rain or shine. In the winter he'd keep a stove stoked bright while he watched the snow fall. He kept his money hidden in an old grease bucket, figuring that nobody would ever look there. Apparently, he was right.

Pap died during the Great Depression, on August 15, 1935. He had been out riding his horse and came back, took off the saddle, and "just lay down." He lay there for about a week and finally died just a month short of his eightieth birthday. He is buried west of Wardville, near where he had his spread.

CHAPTER 5

Pap didn't care much for rodeos and Wild West shows and the like. But his son John was captured by the cowboy's life. When it came to stopping John from chasing rodeos, Pap was helpless as a frozen snake.

Pap was a "slave driver" with his kids, Ray Williams recalls, "but he never could do nothin' with John." John always had the true cowboy spirit: too proud to cut hay, but not quite wild enough to eat it.

Early on, John left home and would come back only once or twice a year "full of stories." John, a great storyteller, kept the family enthralled with his adventures with the rodeo and traveling.

John cost the family plenty of money. There wasn't any money to be made in rodeo, so John kept borrowing all the money he could off anyone who would lend it to him. When he got back home, he'd always round up some pigs or guineas or whatever else he could, and sell them without telling anyone else. John never called it stealing, it was always "poochin'." When word came that John was going to visit, Pap would always tell the family, "Better watch your horses and stuff. John's going to be around for a while."

When John came home, his family remembers, he'd spend all his time roping when he wasn't telling stories. He'd rope anything that moved, and if nothing was moving, he'd rope just anything at all. If John had gotten a nickle for every time he tossed a rope, he'd have died the richest man in the world.

When John was born, the Wild West shows were more popular and better organized than the rodeos, and he joined the 101

Ranch Wild West Show when it came through the area. It was with the 101 Ranch Wild West Show that he went to Madison Square Garden in New York.

After being with the Wild West Show, he tried his hand at winning some money with his rope, entering his first roping contest at Pittsburg, Oklahoma, in 1914, when he was seventeen.

There weren't many automobiles at the time John started rodeoing; even if there were, they wouldn't have been able to travel on most of the roads in Oklahoma and the West, because most roads weren't much more than trails. And horse trailers weren't even an idea yet. So when John took out for a rodeo, he did it on his saddle horse, usually leading a pack horse if he didn't have too far to go. When he did have a long ride—say, two hundred miles—he brought a wagon hooked to a team. In that wagon was horse feed and his camping gear.

Rodeos didn't always have calves and steers to rope; sometimes the cowboys roped goats. At one rodeo where John McEntire roped, they came up short of goats. The next year John hauled a wagon full of goats to that rodeo.

In June 1925 John married twenty-four-year-old Alice Kate Hayhurst. Alice and John had grown up in the same area; in fact, Alice's father and Pap McEntire were supposedly in the same horse-stealing outfit. But the Hayhursts never did cotton to John McEntire, resented his marrying their daughter, and held it against him his whole life.

Alice had been to college and got a degree. According to one old-timer, "John was waiting at the door when she got that degree, and as soon as she walked off that stage he took her right out and married her. Wouldn't wait. She had that paycheck, see, from teaching school."

It was Alice's paycheck that let John keep rodeoing. He loved that rodeo, and was good at it, too. He had started out riding bucking broncs, had been one of the earliest bulldoggers, and wound up a champion roper.

On November 30, 1927, John and Alice's son, Clark, was born.

15

That was also the year John started raising cattle on a ranch near Kiowa. But then came the Great Depression—actually, the West felt the blow before the stock market crash back East in October 1929—so John hit the rodeo trail again.

A good roper, John won the steer-roping contest up in Cheyenne in 1934. At that time, if you won in Cheyenne you were considered world champion, so the records list John McEntire as champion steer roper for that year. The next year, 1935, he won both the bulldogging and calf-roping events in Shreveport, Louisiana. Later he won steer-roping contests in Ada, Seminole, and Pawhuska, Oklahoma. He traveled as far north as Wolf Point, Montana, and even roped one year in Madison Square Garden in New York.

John was fortunate to marry Alice, because her income—she taught first grade down in Cairo—allowed him to go chasing after rodeos. She is described as a "big, fleshy woman" who weighed between 250 and 300 pounds, and the two apparently had a happy marriage.

Their house, located about a quarter-mile from the Limestone Gap School, had a dirt floor in part of it and a single lamp. John, never the model home handyman, let a lot of things slide in the fixing-up department. But he always had plenty of time to tell stories, entertain kids and cowboys, go to a rodeo, or throw a rope.

In 1950, the year his wife died, John McEntire hung up his rodeo rope at the age of fifty-three. That same year he had won at Pendleton, Oregon, and his last trip to the pay window had occurred in Woodward, Oklahoma.

When Alice died, "it just about did in John. He was pathetic, 'cause he depended on her for everything." John had a hard time making ends meet his whole life, and now that Alice was gone, well, it was a real struggle. But that didn't stop him from being a "cowboy character" until his last breath.

CHAPTER 6

A statue of Buffalo Bill Cody sits atop Persimmon Hill in Oklahoma City in front of the National Cowboy Hall of Fame. The nineteen-foot statue depicts Buffalo Bill rearing up on his horse, his right hand holding his rifle high in the air, beckoning toward the West, inviting one and all to be part of the grand adventure of the frontier. It is appropriate that Buffalo Bill is here, because more than any other single person, he is responsible for popularizing the cowboy and the West, making the cowboy an American hero and myth.

The first non-native people to explore and inherit the West were adventurers, explorers, trappers, mountain men, and gold seekers. The cowboy did not really come along until after the Civil War, around 1867, when America answered the call of Manifest Destiny and spread from sea to shining sea.

The first stories of the West were told in dime novels by writers like Ned Buntline (whose real name was Edward Judson), Colonel Prentiss Ingraham, Samuel S. Hall, Gerald Carlton, and others. The eastern public, curious about the western frontier, had grown tired of the stories of Davy Crockett and Daniel Boone, the two earlier heroes. Eager readers of fictional tales of the West, which contained a little fact and a lot of fancy, believed the dime novels' stereotypes and romantic notions of what it was like to be a cowboy out West. By the 1870s the cowboy was an important character in popular American literature.

The first time Easterners heard of William Frederick Cody, better known as Buffalo Bill, was in a dime novel by Ned Buntline. Buntline had gone west in search of fresh material for his novels and run across Buffalo Bill, already a legend among Westerners.

In his youth, Cody had lived the life he later dramatized in his Wild West shows. He had battled Indians, been a Pony Express rider, fought in the Civil War, been an Army scout, and worked for a freighting firm and the railroad, killing buffalos (he reportedly killed 4,280 in eighteen months, cutting off the hump and hindquarters and leaving the rest to rot).

The seeds for his Wild West show were planted in the summer of 1882, when Cody returned to his hometown of North Platte, Nebraska, and headed up the Fourth of July celebration. For that event he started the "Old Glory Blowout." He also rounded up prizes from local businessmen for some roping, shooting, riding, and bronco-breaking events, hoping to attract about a hundred cowboy contestants. He got a thousand, and thus began professional rodeo as we know it today.

From the following year, 1883, until 1916, a much-expanded traveling version of the Old Glory Blowout, billed as Buffalo Bill's Wild West, toured the eastern United States and Europe, including performances at the Chicago World's Fair in 1893. Committed to authenticity, Cody avoided the word *show*, referring to his production as an "exhibition."

Audiences at Buffalo Bill's Wild West saw depictions of an attack on the Deadwood mail coach, a Pony Express ride, a buffalo hunt, and, in the traditional finale, Custer's Last Stand. A segment entitled "Cowboy Fun" included attempts to ride wild broncs and mules.

In bronc riding, the cowboys had to mount their animals out in the open—there were no chutes, and usually the beasts were thrown to the ground so the cowboy could get on—and stay on the bucking animal until either the animal quit bucking or the cowboy hit the ground. There were also some steer-wrestling events and the roping and riding of "Texas Wild Steers."

The genius of Buffalo Bill's show was that it took the cowboy away from working cows and made him a hero, a star performer amid the trappings of the wild West. Instead of hired hands engaged in the usually boring and often dangerous work of herding cattle, Buffalo Bill's cowboys were rootin' tootin' adventurers, the embodiment of a new American myth.

CHAPTER 7

Although Buffalo Bill Cody is the person most responsible for popularizing the cowboy as an American hero, he did not do it alone. In 1902 Owen Wister, a Harvard graduate who had visited the West, wrote *The Virginian*, which established the gunfight as a western set piece and gave us the line "When you call me that, smile!" The novel sold more than 1.5 million copies. Soon Frederick Schiller Faust (who used a number of pen names, including Max Brand) and a New York dentist named Zane Grey were also writing popular novels of the West. Those writers, along with painter and sculptor Frederic Remington and Rough-Rider-turned-President Teddy Roosevelt, all contributed to the myth of the West and the cowboy.

More specifically, Buffalo Bill popularized what would become known as professional rodeo. Still, he certainly did not invent the rodeo. The roots for that event came from the working life of the cowboy in the period between 1867 and 1893, the time when cowboys were a real, integral part of the American West.

The cattle industry came about on the Great Plains at that time because the long stretches of grass there could support large herds of cattle. By great good fortune, those cattle herds happened to be there already, the property of anyone who would round them up.

The cattle were Texas longhorns, originally brought over by the Spanish. When the Spanish had left the area, some cattle stayed, and those animals' descendants developed, untended by man. The result was cattle that required little care and attention, that possessed long, sharp horns for defense, that were capable of enduring harsh extremes in weather, that had low water requirements, and whose rough, wiry, long-legged frames could endure long trail drives.

The big problem was how to get these cattle to market. The incentive was good: a four-dollar steer on the range became a forty-dollar steer when it got to market, so a number of entrepreneurs were willing to gamble. The problem was partially solved by the railroads, which had been laying rails to connect the country and on whose cars the cattle could be transported to eastern cities. It was also partially solved by the development of "cow towns" like Abilene and Chicago, which developed a whole industry of buying cattle, processing them, and shipping the beef east.

Back East, there were plenty of buyers. Beef used to be available only to kings and the rich; with the abundance of longhorns in the West, that meat was now available to the everyday American. The result was that Americans became the largest consumers of beef in the world and the quintessential American food became the hamburger.

The way to get the cattle to market was to hire men on horseback to herd the cattle from the Great Plains to the markets. The men who engaged in this tedious job of standing watch over cattle were called "cowpunchers" because of the long poles they used to keep cattle on their feet and moving.

Trail drives presented numerous dangers—stampedes, cattle rustlers, and renegade Indians, not to mention the land itself, whose vast open spaces, dotted with prairie dog holes, carried a threat of quick, violent storms, flash floods, whirlpools, and quicksand. The cowboy had to ride for hours, even days at a time, without food or rest.

The nature of the cowboy's work bound him to a unique and distinctive society. The result was men who felt immense pride in being cowboys and reveled in their adventures while disdaining the lives of farmers, city slickers, merchants, and anyone else who wasn't out riding the range.

Along the way, the cowboy developed a look as well. The big, wide-brimmed cowboy hat shaded him from the sun and gave him protection from the rain, snow, wind, and dust. It also served as a signal flag to wave and a whip to spur his mount. The hat could hold food or water for his horse and could serve as a gathering basket, a campfire fan, or even a pillow. Boots, with their high heels, helped the cowboy stay in the saddle as well as dig in the ground when he had his rope around a steer. Their high sides protected him from dreaded rattlesnakes.

The horse became not only a way to get around but a true friend as well. Out in the wide open spaces, a man on foot was doomed; a cowboy needed a horse in order to survive. Along the way, he developed a closeness with and interdependency on his horse that led him to disdain walking and consider the horse as much a part of himself as his own legs.

Spending so much time alone on the plains with cattle, in a life filled with endless hours of boredom as well as danger, it is inevitable that the cowboy would want to socialize and maybe let off some steam when he got the chance.

When cowboys got together at the end of the day or the end of a trail drive, or on a holiday like the Fourth of July, they might engage in cards, dominoes, or other gambling games. But these were physical men, used to an active, outdoor existence, so it is only natural they would entertain themselves with things like tossing down steers, roping calves, and riding broncs—activities that were an extension of their everyday life.

It is significant that those men did not engage in foot races or wrestling matches. Such activities didn't involve a horse or cow, and every worthwhile activity, whether work or play, needed to involve horses and cows. These were people whose whole existence, whose whole talk and way of life, was intimately connected with cattle and horses.

Bronc-riding contests were first held in Deer Trail, Colorado, in 1869, an outgrowth of a rivalry between two outfits. A steer-roping contest took place in the early 1880s on the main street in Pecos, Texas, and in 1872 Cheyenne, Wyoming, saw an exhibition of Texas steer-riding.

In 1888 a fairly well-organized contest was held in Prescott,

Arizona, where admission was charged and prizes given. Because this city claims to have awarded the earliest rodeo trophy and because it hosts the longest-running continual annual rodeo in America, the Prescott rodeo lays claim to the title of "Grand-daddy of 'Em All."

In the late 1880s and early 1890s a number of Western towns held rodeos as public events, and the rodeo increasingly became a spectator sport. Along the way, some of the big ones came into being: Frontier Days in Cheyenne, Wyoming, in 1897, the Pendleton Roundup in Oregon in 1911, and the Calgary Stampede in Alberta, Canada, in 1912.

As the twentieth century progressed, rodeo became big business. The Rodeo Association of America, formed by the management groups of several rodeos, began in 1929. In 1936 came the Cowboys' Turtle Association (so named because "we were slow as turtles doin' somethin' like this") to organize rodeo performers. This latter group was renamed the Rodeo Cowboys' Association in 1945 and then, in 1975, the Professional Rodeo Cowboys' Association.

CHAPTER 8

Clark McEntire, Reba's daddy, was born in Graham, Oklahoma, near Ada, and started roping early in life, entering his first amateur roping contest in Ada when he was twelve, in 1939. He had to borrow a horse from a friend, Dick Truitt, and another friend, Eddie Curtis, had paid the three-dollar entry fee. After all that, Clark missed his steer.

By the age of sixteen Clark was competing professionally; at seventeen he joined the Rodeo Cowboys' Association, the pros' organization. Regularly winning some money with his rope, he acquired the nickname "Ropentire" along the way.

In 1947, at nineteen, Clark won the roping event at the Pendleton Round Up. In 1949 he finished fifth in overall steer-roping earnings, making $1,222 with his rope that year. He didn't finish in the top five again until 1953, and the following year he finished second to Shoat Webster. In 1955, the year Reba was born, Clark finished third among steer ropers. In 1957 he finished first with winnings of $5,184—which would be his biggest year ever.

In 1958, when he won the National Steer Roping Championship saddle, he won $3,314, and in 1961, when he was tops in earnings again as well as champ, he won $3,877. But after 1969, when he won $2,615, Clark never finished in the top money again.

When Clark McEntire won his first steer-roping title in 1958, he and his daddy became the first father and son ever to win that championship. That was the same year he won the steer-roping buckle at Cheyenne.

When Clark won the National Steer Roping Championship for the third time in 1961, it was the closest title race he'd ever been in. Going into the Laramie Finals at the end of September, Clark had a $627 lead. (In rodeo, the "points" are the dollars the cowboy has won.) He was riding Earl Corbin's horse Heel Fly, the same horse he'd ridden at the finals the year before.

The event in Wyoming started out in cold, wintry weather on September 22. On that first day, Clark took 35.9 seconds to get his steer down, then missed his first toss at the second one, finally tying him in 34.9. After that weak performance, his lead had dwindled to $270. Going for the sixth steer, only two seconds separated three men in the event—young Joe Snively of Pawhuska, Oklahoma, whose father, Jim Snively, had won the title in 1956, former title-holder Shoat Webster of Lenapah, Oklahoma, and defending champ Don McLaughlin. Any one of three men could win the overall steer-roping title for the year: Clark, Snively, or Webster.

The weather warmed up on the third day. In the fifth and last go-round, Snively tied his steer in 18.6, while Webster tied his in 23.3. Clark came through, tying his steer in 19.8 seconds, to

23

win the national championship by only $94 over Snively, who won the Laramie Finals contests, and Webster, who won high money that year at Laramie.

Clark is heavyset—in 1961 he carried 225 pounds on his five-foot-eleven frame—but was surprisingly quick and agile in his roping days. In his career he won just about every major steer-roping contest in the rodeo world, and his time of 14.5 seconds on a single steer was a record he held for several years. Outside the rodeo ring he moved slow and easy, with a quiet, easygoing demeanor, but inside the ring he was a fierce competitor, relentlessly consistent in his roping and remarkably fast getting off his horse and covering the ground to his steer.

In addition to steer roping, Clark was also a formidable calf and team roper. In team roping, one roper throws his loop over the head while the other roper, trailing the steer, must rope the hind legs. Then the two ropers stretch the steer out once he's down, holding him for the judge.

In roping contests the luck of the draw, always crucial, is the one factor that puts the roper at the mercy of fate. Sometimes the steer is fast and the cowboy must spend extra precious seconds on his horse chasing him down; other times the steer or calf might turn and run toward the fence, or stop while the cowboy is going full tilt, or twist and turn instead of running straight, or have an uncanny knack of ducking just as the rope is in the air. You want a steer to run in a straight line and at a steady speed, not too fast, but that's not always what you get.

John McEntire impressed upon Clark the need to practice his roping constantly. He once told the boy, "Son, regardless of what happens, if the well goes dry or the house catches fire, you keep right on practicing. Your mother and I will put it out." At the height of his success Clark was asked the most important element for success as a roper. He replied, "Practice, practice, practice." He considered rodeo his hobby as well as his work and for his future wanted "more rodeo, more cattle, more land."

By the end of 1961 Clark was at the top of his form but road weary. He roped for money and put the money he won into land and his ranch. He eventually owned seven thousand acres and leased more to graze his cattle.

Clark McEntire had grown up in Kiowa and attended the Limestone Gap School. He married Jacqueline Smith on March 17, 1950, at the First Baptist Church in Atoka.

Their first child, Alice Lynn, was born in December the following year. Next came Dale Stanley, also called Pecos Pete and nicknamed Pake, in June 1953, then Reba Nell in March 1955, and finally, Martha Susan, called Susie, in November 1957.

Jackie also came from a rodeo family and understood that life. She came from that area—south of Kiowa near Atoka—and had taught school. Jackie's parents were hardworking country people, and her grandmother was a Brasfield from McAlester. She was a distant relative—a second or third cousin—of the country comedian Rod Brasfield.

With her beautiful singing voice, Jackie made sure there was always music in the McEntire house. While their daddy gave them a rich heritage of ranching and rodeo life, it was from their mother that the kids inherited their musical ability, and it was she who taught them songs, taught them harmony, and always pushed them toward the stage.

CHAPTER 9

It seems to be a telling fact that most of those involved in traditional country music have rural or small-town backgrounds. In fact, the five most significant and influential country acts to emerge in the 1980s—Alabama, George Strait, Ricky Skaggs, Randy Travis, and Reba McEntire—all come from rural or small-town backgrounds. This comes at a time when we are bombarded with news that we are an urban nation, that everybody lives in cities, that all the things that matter happen in cities. And sitting in Nashville—the country music capital of the world, with a population of about a million—it is easy to believe that. But country music is rooted in rural America, and despite the statistics and stories, there still is a rural and small-town America out there. And the country stars come from those places. So do the country fans.

The ones who don't, the ones who are living in cities, somehow still have these rural roots and values, still believe in honor and patriotism and God. The anonymity of the big city—where anybody can do anything and get away with it, where nobody can nosy into your business, where nobody is accountable, where everything is available and tacitly accepted—has not eaten up the hearts, souls, and minds of all those who live in small towns. Country music represents the heart of America, which is still rural and small town. Big cities are just where most people are; it's not where they live.

Living in southeastern Oklahoma—in Kiowa or Atoka or Stringtown or Chockie—you get used to driving a lot to get anywhere. Tulsa is about three hours north, Oklahoma City about three hours west-northwest, and Dallas about three hours south. When you're traveling to rodeos you get used to the roads that lead out of this area.

State Routes 69 and 75 are the same road, a wide four-lane that runs through the area. If you're traveling south from McAlester, you'd better gas up good because there's a lot of road with few gas stops between there and the state line. In the stretch from Kiowa to Atoka—about twenty-five miles—there's hardly a gas station around. You've got to watch closely how near that needle is to the *E* on the gas gauge in this piece of the world.

Heading north out of Kiowa, the four-lane turns into Route 75 at McAlester and takes you into Tulsa. It's pretty much a straight shot, long stretches of nothing but white-line fever with Oklahoma running along beside the blacktop. The limestone hills of Atoka, Stringtown, and Chockie give way to flat land as you travel north before you hit Tulsa and then the rolling hills of Claremore and northeastern Oklahoma.

Back in southeastern Oklahoma, a lot of the roads aren't paved, once you get off that black ribbon—just crushed limestone, a dark gray gravel. You need to have high-suspension vehicles—there aren't many of those sleek little sports cars hung low to hug the ground around here. Most people go for pickup trucks, the contemporary cowboy's horse, built high, tough, and strong.

The population of Kiowa is listed at 754, and it's mostly poor. That big, black four-lane carrying traffic zooming by all day and all night from Tulsa to Dallas cuts through the area, so those living there hear a lot of cars and trucks and see plenty of plates from other states. But few of those driving through stop in Kiowa, except maybe for gas or a hamburger.

Those who do stop find only a few gas pumps and not a big variety in the eats department. There are no Chinese restaurants here; vegetarians won't find much on the menu and should not advertise their inclinations. This is cattle country, and these are meat-and-potatoes people.

Order a hamburger here and you get a big one; finish one and it feels like a McDonald's is about the size of a quarter. They don't weigh the meat with little plastic bags wrapped around their hands to make you feel you're getting your money's worth—getting the same amount as the billion before you and the billion to come after. No sir, they grab that meat and make it into a patty, and you know you're being treated right. It's a code here—you treat others right and you know they'll treat you right. Slap that meat on the bun and be assured that no two are exactly alike and be glad of it. Individualism even applies to the hamburgers.

Not everybody wears a cowboy hat and boots here. A lot of men wear caps and tennis shoes. But just about every man wears jeans; cowboys don't wear shorts or cutoffs, no matter how hot it is. Most have a tanned, ruddy complexion, evidence of spending a lot of time outside. It is not considered impolite to eat with your hat on.

27

Straddling the four-lane is the real Kiowa, spread out on each side. Route 63 east is a winding, narrow two-lane that carries you off to the high school. To the west is the narrow two-lane of the town: a post office, city hall, barbershop, fire department, grocery store, a couple of stores with locks on the door and junk inside—broken furniture and stacked boxes behind dirty windows.

This is Reba McEntire's hometown (although she actually grew up on a ranch about ten miles south), and coming into Kiowa from the north there's a big sign announcing that fact. "Home of Reba McEntire," it says, "Female C.M.A. Vocalist of the Year 1984–1985–1986–1987." But while Reba's name is the biggest one on that billboard, the area seems just as proud of her rodeo relatives. Beneath Reba's name are those of her granddaddy, John McEntire; her daddy, Clark McEntire; cousin Don Smith; and Bill Hensley, all of whom found fame as champion rodeo cowboys.

Growing up in a small place like this amid such poverty can be excruciatingly lonely, numbingly boring. In the days before TV and radio, people used to ache to have someone to talk with, or just to see another person. It was a lonely group who first moved west and pushed the frontier westward. That life was particularly difficult for women. The menfolk would get with other cowboys on a cattle drive, or go into town for supplies, but most women in the early West stayed home to look after the kids and the place. They had to protect the home, tend the garden, do washing by hand, and fix meals without electricity, refrigerators, or microwaves.

There are no movie theaters in Kiowa or in most of these small towns. This is largely attributed to the Baptists' aversion to movie theaters—dens of sin where young folks might do forbidden things in the dark. And those movies could be dangerous to morals, too. Ironically, the same movies are safe when they're in your living room; parents have grown accustomed to watching movies on TV they would forbid their kids to see in a theater. There are places to rent videotapes in Kiowa, and unless you're willing to drive about thirty miles to McAlester, that's how you see movies there.

CHAPTER 10

You can hardly go anywhere in Oklahoma around Kiowa or Atoka—or even up in Claremore or Chelsea or over in Oklahoma City—without running into people who know the McEntires. They are decent, wonderful people who are well known and well liked for their work in rodeos through the years, their community involvement, and their outright friendliness.

People also know the kids, and most have a friendly, funny story about Reba as a kid, about a fun-filled tomboy with red hair and freckles who was down-to-earth, friendly, outgoing, mischievous, and filled with talent. The phrases you hear most often are "She's a ball of fire" and "She was something, she was."

Reba has said of her parents, "They were a very high-standard people expectin' us to have high morals. It was unthinkable to even think about lyin'. And they were very concerned about values ... all that kind of stuff a kid's supposed to know." The McEntire kids made their parents proud, and still do.

The friends of the McEntires are mostly down-to-earth folks. They live everyday lives—shopping in grocery stores and Wal-Marts, watching TV—and they're proud of that. One friend tells a story of getting a shopping cart with a bad wheel everywhere she goes, while another fusses about shopping for a husband who knows exactly what he wants but won't go out and get it himself—won't take it back if she gets it wrong, either. But they all love people, and they're all connected to the day-to-day life of small-town and rural Oklahoma.

29

When Clark McEntire wasn't out on the rodeo circuit, he was on his ranch, working cattle. Reba's mom, Jackie, had a job as secretary to Harold Toaz, Kiowa's school superintendent, during the time the McEntire kids were growing up.

Reba was a tomboy, always envying Pake for being a boy. "I always wanted to mow yards, haul hay, do tomboy stuff," she says. "Daddy always told me if I'd go back in there and practice my music, that would make me more money than rodeoin' or haulin' hay."

The concern with money and the children's future was always on the parents' minds. Reba says, "Daddy pushed us toward singin', didn't want us to be out on the road with rodeo all the time, but Mama hauled us to rodeos, playdays, 4-H, and any showdeos goin'." She adds, "Daddy didn't want us to rodeo. He knew we had other talents somewhere else, and he didn't want us to waste it."

Of course, the music they listened to and sang was country music. It's just part of the ranching life, part of living in rural Oklahoma. "Bein' grazin' people and bein' around rodeos, country-western was all we ever thought about singin'," says Reba. "I never said 'I'm gonna be a country singer.' It's just something I did."

Reba didn't need a lot of pushing to get on the stage. "I've always wanted to sing," she says. "I've sung all my life, and I've always wanted to be up onstage and get that attention. I was the third of four kids, and the third child never got much attention. That's the way it always happens. So it worked out that the only time I got any attention was when I was singin'. I liked it; it was the only thing I could do very well that I felt comfortable with."

But the ranching life gave her a strong heritage and good memories. "Some of my fondest memories are of mornings when Daddy would get us kids up and Grandpap would come over to the house," she says. "We were up long before the sun ever thought about comin' over the hill. We'd take off to the north end and gather cattle and bring 'em back toward the house. It was so dark comin' back in at night that when the horses' feet would strike rocks, you could see the sparks. It was an all-day affair, and you just barely ever got off the horse except to eat dinner. And that was just a little sack lunch—a cold baloney sandwich."

Reba remembers the competitiveness of her childhood. "Alice was two years older than Pake, Pake was two years older than me, and I was two and a half years older than Susie. So me and Pake, bein' in the middle, were very close. We were a lot alike, and very competitive. So we were always havin' fistfights. Like, in the mornings, Daddy would send us out to go catch the horses and saddle 'em up before daylight. Daddy would cook breakfast, and all of us kids would stumble in there and eat, and then we'd be takin' out for the north end before the sun came up. I mean, it was real dark and cold.

"This was in the fall roundup, to weigh cattle. And me and Pake in the middle of the day, when we're tired and hot and had already pinned one bunch and were goin' after another, if we had to sit and wait for somebody, we'd usually wind up in a big fistfight—on horses! You know, 'Get off that horse and I'll go ahead and whup you, and we'll settle this right quick!' Things like that. But if anybody else ever stepped in, it was us two against them.

"Then when we were in the house, if we were ever bored, it was a competitive thing—anything you can do, I can do better. It would start off, 'I can throw a rock farther than you can.' 'Well, I can sing better than you!' 'Well, I can play guitar better than you.' 'Well, I can play the piano better than you can!' So I was very competitive and very much a tomboy."

Although Reba preferred being out on a horse on the range with the cattle, a woman's job was to cook. One day, while the McEntires were out working, Clark sent Reba back to the house to fix a bite of dinner. Reba drummed up what she could: a meal of beans. There was every kind of bean you could imagine in a bowl: pinto, navy, green. And that was the whole meal—there was no meat on the table, which didn't set well with the menfolk, who like some side meat with their vegetables. Clark complimented her for her cooking anyway, but he never forgot the meal.

The McEntire kids were born into the rodeo life, and at first they didn't really realize that other people were raised differently. "I didn't know anything else," Reba says. "I thought everybody did it. It was Daddy rodeoin', Grandpap rodeoin', and us four kids takin' out with Mama and Daddy in the car, pullin' horses behind us. It was four kids in the back seat wrestlin' and fightin' and stayin' in hotels and gettin' five hamburgers for a dollar." That traveling took them all across Oklahoma and Texas, to Colorado and north to the high country of Montana and Wyoming, and out to Oregon.

Despite his rodeo winnings, Clark wanted more for his kids. "He wanted more out of life for us," says Reba. "Like maybe bankin' or law, or even drivin' some old bus! So when we took to singin', that tickled him to death."

On the surface, it may seem a little strange that Clark would encourage singing and show business as a secure way to make money, but that's not the way he saw it.

Country music and rodeos have always gone hand in hand. Before a rodeo there's country music coming over the loudspeakers. And after the rodeo there's usually a dance with country music.

If the singer misses a note, he still gets paid; if a roper misses a steer, there's no money to be had. As long as there are rodeos—and the future of that seems pretty assured—then there'll be a demand for country music. And when the rodeos aren't going, like in the winter, well, you can still play country music. With singing and playing, if you show up and play, you get paid, no matter what. It's not like roping, where you have to depend on the luck of the draw.

CHAPTER 11

The McEntire kids took every opportunity to sing, even for friends who dropped by the house. Reba remembers, "When friends of Mama and Daddy would come over and play dominoes or something, me and Pake would get in, and they'd get Pake to sing a song, and I'd do my best to beat Pake out for attention by singin' too. I used singin' in a lot more ways than just makin' money. I like attention."

School was more than just an education for the McEntires. Jackie worked at the school, and those around the school were close friends. Reba's first "official" public performance came at Kiowa School, singing "Away in a Manger" for her first-grade Christmas play.

In the second grade, Reba sang at the senior class graduation ceremony. The speaker for that event was Carl Albert, the Speaker of the House of Representatives. When Reba was finished singing, Congressman Albert, in a prophetic statement, announced, "Ladies and gentlemen, one day that young lady's name will be more famous than her father's."

Clark Rhyne has been a teacher at Kiowa High School since December 1965. He had gotten out of college in the spring of 1965 and had worked for the Naval Ammunition Depot before he heard of the opening at the school. Clark Rhyne goes back a long way with the McEntires: his grandfather's sister was Alice Buié, Pap McEntire's first wife. And he grew up around Wardville, near where Pap had his spread.

In 1969 Clark was teaching art and history. Jackie wanted her kids to have a musical outlet at school, which had no marching band. So she cooked up the idea of having a country music band with the school kids and enlisted Clark Rhyne's support.

Clark had grown up loving country music. On Christmas 1954 he had received a fiddle and "took to it like a duck to water." In six months he "knew every old fiddle tune." But by the time he was in high school, it wasn't cool to play fiddle; all the young bucks had guitars slung over their shoulders. So Clark learned the guitar and played in bands.

In 1959, while still in high school, Clark began playing at the Kiowa Dance, a Saturday-night event that featured western swing and Texas honky-tonk music. He joined Smiley Weaver, who'd worked with Bob Wills and the Miller brothers, at the beginning of 1964. They played at the W H Corral in Sulphur. He was playing this gig on weekends when Reba was in school.

The big obstacle was Jackie's boss, school superintendant Harold Toaz. He had to be convinced. No problem—Jackie could handle that and make it come out seeming like it was his idea. And so it was done.

Harold wanted to know how much all this would cost. The figure that was reached was "less than a thousand dollars." He also was adamant that the band play country music, and not that loud, noisy rock 'n' roll. Rhyne took the money and purchased a public address system, a bass, amplifiers, and some other equipment. Soon the group was practicing during the morning, and within two or three weeks the Kiowa Cowboy Band had fifteen or twenty songs ready, having learned them out of songbooks.

There was a slight problem within the group concerning musical tastes. The McEntires were definitely into country, but some of the others—like Roger Wills, Gary Rayburn, David Jones, and Kelly Rhyne (Clark's younger brother)—were into rock 'n' roll. But all of them knew that if they wanted to play in the band, they'd have to play country. So they knuckled under, but not without a bit of grumbling now and then.

And they didn't stop listening to rock. Kelly, Reba's high school boyfriend, introduced her to Three Dog Night and Chicago albums, and she remembers loving the harmonies she heard.

Running the band was a battle of nerves for Clark Rhyne, keeping the rockers happy and making sure the community accepted it, not to mention keeping himself happy. He managed to do so because of the rare group of youngsters in that class. "You couldn't find another group like that in forty years," says Clark. "It was just a miracle that they were all together in this school at the same time." In fact, every one of those involved in that class has made a living from country music.

The school building would inevitably be packed when the group played concerts there. They would play at 4-H events, football halftimes, clubs, fairs, and talent contests whenever they could. In their first year they went to the Muskogee Fair and won top prize singing "Okie from Muskogee."

As a matter of fact, the McEntires won so many talent contests that the judges gave the group a Reserve Championship once just so somebody else could win. In 1971 Reba won a talent contest in Atoka, and her prize was the use of a Ford Torino for six months. Trouble was, Reba didn't have any money for gas. Clark Rhyne had a wife and one-year-old baby, so he made Reba a deal: if she'd supply the car, he'd buy the gas. The deal was made and the group—Clark, his wife, baby Jim, Reba, and Reba's friend Debbie Boyd—took off for Colorado and the Rockies. They spent about ten days out there, seeing Pike's Peak and the other sights and putting on a load of miles.

The group played a number of dates all over southeastern Oklahoma. Reba remembers, "Pake sang lead; Susie and me sang harmony. They didn't say we couldn't go out and make money. Mama used to take us to every one. Then we'd crawl in the back seat and just sleep all the way home. Our feet were killin' us; our throats were hurtin'; our eyes were burnin' from the smoke in those little clubs. We were just little kids."

One of the places the Kiowa Cowboy Band played was the Sports Arena in Ada, Oklahoma, at the dances organized by Ken Lance. For these, Reba and the other members of the band would get thirteen dollars each for playing from nine at night until two in the morning.

The band began to unravel in 1971, when Pake graduated from high school. Then the next year, several more of the band members graduated, and that seemed to end it. "People thought it was like a basketball team," said Clark Rhyne. "That when somebody left, somebody else would go into that slot. But that bunch was talented, and you couldn't find any others to replace them." By the time Reba graduated in 1973 it was obvious to all who heard them practice that the replacements in this little music class wouldn't draw much of a crowd if they played in public.

Reba and the group had their first recording session in 1971 when the McEntires went to Benson Recording Studio in Oklahoma City to record "The Ballad of John McEntire." Clark Rhyne had written the song in about an hour on a Sunday afternoon —"I just took the guitar down from the wall and started playing, and the words rolled out, 'Gather round me boys,' and the way it came was like it was given to me." The next day Clark played it for the McEntires. They wanted a verse about their Grandma Alice in there, so Clark added one, and in the middle of the week they recorded it.

Originally, Jackie was going to sing harmony, but as they were running the song down, the engineer noted that two of the singers had the same part. So Jackie went into the control room and the kids sang it.

On the B side was the McEntire kids interviewing their Grandpa John. A thousand copies were pressed on Boss Records and sold to whoever wanted to buy one.

On August 27, 1971, Clark took a group back to the Benson Recording Studio to record some more songs he'd written. Reba sang one of these: "Johnny." A little later, this group evolved into the Singing McEntires—Pake, Reba, and Susie singing together at rodeos. As Reba notes, "Whenever anybody at a rodeo wanted some singin', we were Johnny-on-the-spot."

Like thousands of other kids, Reba grew up in a life filled with school and community activities. In high school she was in 4-H and on the basketball team, which went to the state finals. People remember her as a scrappy, aggressive player. The kids were active in junior rodeos, school activities, and other community events.

A good student, Reba graduated salutatorian. Clark Rhyne remembers, "She wasn't part of any crowd, but she got along with all of them—the rodeo kids and the basketball kids and the bookworms. She was always her own person." Even at that age she had the overwhelming personality that created an instant rapport with whomever she met; she could always get along with anybody.

A family with four kids is a busy family, always going somewhere, doing something, involved in thousands of things. Each kid has friends, those friends have parents, and those parents have friends; the kids all go to one another's houses to play, and the parents run into one another in town or at school functions, until a huge interlocking network is formed of people who know one another, know one another's kids, and are involved somehow in one another's lives. If you have four kids, you get to know a lot of people.

And so most folks in the Kiowa area have run into Reba and the McEntire family at some time in their lives.

CHAPTER 12

There are First Baptist churches in Kiowa, Stringtown, and Atoka. In fact, the Baptists were in Oklahoma as early as 1869, when J. S. Morrow and five others came to this area as missionaries to the Indians. Reverend Morrow established the Morrow Indian Orphan's Home in 1913 and some of the first schools, as well as the first Baptist association in Oklahoma.

The Baptists are a folky sect, known for their intense concern for souls—their own as well as everyone else's. At their worst,

Baptists can be intolerant and nosy, inflicting their views and interpretation of God's will on the world; at their best they are kind, loving, considerate, and generous, reaching out to those in need and making sure people are looked after and taken care of. They want to know what everybody else is doing, and they share what they are doing with others. You don't keep secrets to yourself for long in a small Baptist church. These people are quick to help you when you need it and equally quick to let you know when they feel you are backsliding or going astray. More than anything, they are concerned for the welfare of individual souls; to that end, they try to influence their community to eliminate temptations to sin while encouraging a church-centered lifestyle. It is a difficult task in a pluralistic world that tends to shun accountability to others in exchange for the anonymity of city life, where what you do is nobody else's business and other people's troubles and cares are none of yours.

These First Baptist churches are generally small groups with one or two hundred core members. The men tend to wear jeans, cowboys boots, and open-necked western shirts to church; even the preacher doesn't wear a tie. The baptismal is at the front, beneath a wooden cross. Wooden pews with padded seats flank a wide center aisle, and the floor is usually covered with an orangish carpet. Walking into a Baptist church, you get the impression Baptists, who are fiercely independent, with a deep, inherent distrust of a central authority, have somehow agreed —not an easy accomplishment in Baptist circles—on a universal orange motif for their decor.

The pastor's lectern usually stands in the center of a raised area in the front; behind are some pews where a group—you can't really call it a choir—sets the example for singing along with the music minister. Like most congregations, out front a few sing full-voiced while the rest stare at hymnals, look around at who else is there, move their lips now and then, or occasionally mumble along with the morning's hymns. After the hymn singing, the group behind the preacher leaves their seats and joins their family and friends in the congregation.

38

In the front on one side of the preacher there's an upright piano and a pianist playing those full, ten-finger chords that are an integral part of the sound of Baptist music making. Also in the front is an organ. When the pianist or organist is not playing, or the preacher is not preaching, or the music minister is not leading the singing, they sit in the congregation. This is a group that believes fully in equality, in little ornamentation or anything that causes them to be set apart from one another. They believe we are all equal in God's eyes, none better than the other, and they set up their churches accordingly.

The Baptists are a musical group, and their love of singing is as vital to their faith and services as the preaching. But the center of the service is the preaching—direct, straightforward, and without reservation, stating forcefully the faith and the message that all should accept it. A man only needs the call of God to be a preacher; that's all the congregation demands and that's what they get. The best preach fire.

At the altar call, people regularly go forward to be saved or perhaps recommit their lives, make a vow to change their ways and have a closer walk with God.

Reba McEntire has been in these Baptist churches and sat in these pews as a girl growing up. She came with her family each week, and the congregation watched those kids grow up, knowing what they were up to, rejoicing in their achievements, sympathizing with their difficulties, interested and concerned about their lives. This was an important part of Reba McEntire's upbringing, and she's never forgotten those Baptist roots. Those kind of roots runs deep in a person's life and affect what they think, say, and do.

Reba said early in her career, "Religion is very important to me. I'm not fanatic or anything, but it is definitely in my roots. I wake up each morning and thank the Lord for all he's done and thank him each night when I go to bed. I want to do well in my music career, but more importantly I want to keep from ever doin' anything that would make him ashamed of me."

To a reporter who asked her once about her future, she said,

"God only knows what's next. He's got it planned. I don't and I don't worry about it." To another reporter she said her future is "already written in that Big Book upstairs."

Early in her career, at a Sunday-school session, some of the church members asked her if it wasn't a spiritual conflict of interest to sing country music in nightclubs while being a Christian. Many in the congregation felt she should avoid non-Christians, the idea being that you'll get a white dress dirty in a coal mine. She told them that "show business helps me in my faith." She felt that "those people in nightclubs are dancin' and havin' a good time. I don't know who they are. They may go to church more than I do. Who am I to say I'm better than they are?"

Reba has often sung gospel songs in her show—songs like "I Saw the Light," "I'll Fly Away," and "When the Roll Is Called Up Yonder" as well as songs like "Somebody Up There Likes Me," which was included on her *Live* album. An original gospel number, "I Know I'll Have a Better Day Tomorrow," was released on her *Reba Nell McEntire* album in 1986. That song was originally recorded a number of years before for her *Unlimited* album, but she held it out at the last minute when her producer, Jerry Kennedy, suggested she record a whole gospel album. She still hasn't done that gospel album, though she says she wants to someday.

PART 2

SOMEONE CARES

FOR YOU

CHAPTER *13*

Rodeo is a man's world, and rodeo men aim to keep it that way. Reba was as much a part of this world as she could be, but that was never as much as she wanted to be. Her brother, Pake, could ride and rope and even bulldog if he felt like it, but Reba could only run barrels—the single event in rodeo where women are allowed to participate.

It wasn't always like this. In the early days of rodeo women participated in roping and bronc-riding events. Up in Cheyenne women rode saddle broncs until 1928. In the Rodeo Hall of Fame in Oklahoma City there's a special exhibit on women in rodeo, with pictures of Fannie Sperry Steele, Florence Hughes Randolph, Lorena Trickey Peterson, and Tad Barnes Lucas.

But by the 1930s women were restricted to races and trick riding. It seems the menfolk decided that women were too fragile and might get hurt around those wild animals. It wasn't ladylike either.

That attitude mirrors the western male's attitude toward women. The old cowboys openly scorned and feared women: they were civilizing influences that could tame a man down, make him lose his precious freedom, get him off his beloved horse, and put him in a house. Cause him to throw out his bedroll and make him sleep in a bed where he couldn't see the stars when he looked up.

It's been said that the two things old-time cowboys were most scared of were a decent woman and being set afoot. A true cowboy always liked horses better than women; he knew you could never trust women, fleas, or tenderfoots. A woman's taming a man was the worst thing that could happen to him—marriage was as risky as braiding a mule's tail.

Indeed, the whole cowboy life-style and image is one of masculinity and male bonding, from nightly gatherings around the campfire to herding cattle with all its adventure and dangers. The cowboy has always held a high regard for a real man and true masculinity. One of the ways the cowboy showed his masculinity was by looking out for the fairer sex. He was chivalric and protective, putting women on a pedestal and always tipping his hat to them—and, of course, keeping them out of his life.

The contemporary rodeo world allows women to be rodeo secretaries or barrel racers. But women are rarely seen back behind the chutes or anywhere near the real action. In barrel racing, a gal—as the rodeo folk would refer to her—comes tearing out of the gate on her horse toward a barrel; the horse makes a sharp turn and heads across the ring to a second barrel, then down the rodeo ring and around the final barrel. Then it's a horse race back to the gate, where the gal traditionally pulls up her horse for a short, quick stop. If the whole thing takes more than fifteen seconds or so, she probably won't be in the money at the end of the night.

It's a scary feeling hanging on to a big, powerful quarter horse tearing down the ring. You must make tight turns, close to the barrels, and knees and shins often get cut and scraped. If you hit the barrel, that adds five seconds to the run; if you knock it down, that adds ten. A barrel racer's legs aren't always a pretty sight.

You've also got to have a good horse, fast and quick. If you get one that shys away from barrels and won't take a turn, then you've lost. And you've got to be close to that horse, feel like you and that horse are one as you run that cloverleaf pattern of barrels, then sprint to the finish.

The gals can't wear jeans at the major rodeos; instead they wear brightly colored, well-tailored suits and matching cowgirl hats. Of course the hats always blow off on a fast run. The menfolk always like to watch a pretty gal, but you get the impression they aren't really taking them seriously when it comes their time in the ring. Matter of fact, up in Cheyenne the barrel race is held outside the actual rodeo, with only the championship go-round held within the regular afternoon rodeo performance on the last day.

The one thing about rodeo gals that sets them apart from men contestants is that they are required to ride in the grand entry if the stock contractor requests it. No rodeo cowboy has to put up with that if he doesn't want to.

CHAPTER *14*

Reba loved riding horses and loved the idea of being in a rodeo, so she rode barrels—the only event open to her. But though she loved it, she was never a champion barrel racer.

She admits, "I was never very good at rodeoin'. I ran barrels —barrel raced—and to tell you the truth, I was terrible at it. I never even had a horse of my own. I always rode rejects—Pake's calf-ropin' horse or Daddy's steer-ropin' horse. I made more money sellin' horses I worked with than by winnin'."

One of the problems Reba always faced is that she was nervous when she was on that horse tearing around the barrels. She says, "Strangely enough, a horse can always tell when you're nervous. I was always scared to death in the arena. But in the mountains, when we were ridin' or when I was trainin' a horse, I wasn't nervous at all. I was a better trainer than I was a performer."

The barrel racer in the McEntire family was Alice, the eldest daughter, who was the runner-up at the International Rodeo Association finals in 1971. "Alice is tougher than I am," says Reba. "And she had a lot better horse than I ever had. As a matter of fact, when she was pregnant with her first child, I begged her to let me compete on her horse, Joe Dan. So we went down to the ropin' pen one day, and I got up on ol' Joe Dan and I said, 'Okay, what do I do now?' Alice said, 'Hang on.' Joe Dan saw them barrels—he was a big quarter horse—and he headed for that first barrel. Pow! My head hit his rear end, and I was pullin' on the reins, tryin' to get back up. Around the first barrel we went, and when we got back my hair was wet from the tears, the wind was hittin' my eyes so hard. I said, 'So that's what it's like!' "

Reba did enjoy training horses and preferred geldings. "At a rodeo, there are horses all around you," she observes. "If you've got a stallion who's wantin' to horse around a bit, you've got a mess on your hands. If there's a mare somewhere in heat, you sure got a mess on your hands. So that's always scared me to death. However, I've known girls to have successful stallions and mares that they win on. But I just can't put up with that. It's too aggravatin' to me; I'm nervous enough."

Training and selling horses for rodeo performers can be quite lucrative, and a top-notch horse can fetch a pretty price. "It's astronomical," says Reba. "A good friend of mine turned down fifty thousand dollars for her horse, and the next day the horse died." With rodeos, you're gambling even when you're out of the ring.

Reba had developed a method for training barrel-racing horses. "You've got to learn 'em the pattern," she says. "My theory—well, actually it's my daddy's theory—is that you want to walk 'em around the barrels for ten days and get 'em used to it. Then for another ten days you trot 'em around the barrels. It's a science, and there are a lot of details to it."

Reba knew the traits of a good barrel horse. "First of all is speed. Quarter horses are good for that. Thoroughbreds are for long distances. Short distances are better for quarter horses. They're quick to turn; they have to run hard, turn, run hard, turn. So they've got to be flexible, mobile, and stout. You've got to have a horse with a good rear end on him, lots of muscles where he can push back out again and take that last bound for home."

She did train one horse that was profitable, but she sold it. "I had one horse I'd trained for the barrels. We eventually sold him and the girl who bought him won an awful lot of money on him. But with me, he knew I was nervous, so he'd get nervous."

The saddle for barrel racers is a bit different from a regular working saddle. "It's got high swells," says Reba. "It's got a little seat, and it's real light, with little stirrups. The swells up front are to keep you in the saddle. I've seen the best be thrown over the horse's head. If you're goin' toward that second barrel and it's near the buckin' chutes, there might be somethin' distractin' in there—like a bull. Most horses are scared to death of bulls. So if he sees that bull, he'll duck to the left of that second barrel, and there you go to the right. You're without a horse and saddle—you're on the ground."

Like all the other events in rodeo, you take a gamble when you enter the barrel-racing competition. You have to pay your entry fee, and then you might qualify for the next round—or your horse might not be fast enough, or maybe he just shies away from a barrel. A lot of other factors go into it as well.

"It depends if they're just runnin' barrels," Reba says of competitors. "It depends if their horse is paid for or if they're borrowin' a horse. The best way and the most professional way is trainin' horses, runnin' in competition, developin' a name for yourself, and then sellin' horses to newcomers or other people in the business."

Most of the time Reba had to borrow a horse. Usually, she borrowed her daddy's roping horse. "Daddy had a horse I ran barrels on," she says. "Pake roped steers on him left-handed, and

47

Daddy could get on him and rope steers right-handed. Now that's very complicated, and I don't see how the horse did it. He was a very smart horse. He was relaxed and knew who was on him at the time. Horses are sure not dumb."

As Reba's singing career was beginning and her barrel-racing days were ending, she used to sit in the chute, waiting to ride, and joke with Gail Pesca, one of the top barrel riders. Gail would tell Reba, "I always wanted to be a singer," and Reba would reply, "I'd give anything to win a barrel race." Then Reba would ask, "Do you wanna swap?" Both would grin and say, "Nah."

Reba competed in junior rodeos in high school and college rodeos when she got to college, and though she won some races, she knew she could never be a star on the rodeo circuit in barrel racing. And, being a woman, she couldn't take a shot at any of the other events.

CHAPTER 15

Cowboys and country music have long been connected. From working cowboys to rodeo riders to drugstore cowboys driving pickup trucks, country music is the music of preference. A number of country music performers dress in cowboy regalia, regardless of whether or not they come from the West or even know how to ride a horse. The reason so many of them dress that way goes back to the singing cowboys in the early movies.

With his kinetograph, a crude movie camera, Thomas Edison filmed Buffalo Bill, Annie Oakley, Lost Horse, and Short Bull in 1894 at his studio in West Orange, New Jersey. The short films were shown on kinetoscopes in penny arcades and vaudeville houses as a novelty, along with such fare as a man sneezing and girls dancing.

When the movie industry began, filmmakers discovered they could dress up actors as cowboys, have them shoot and fight, and end up with a pretty good silent movie. The first full-length movie with a plot was *The Great Train Robbery*, a ten-minute film made in 1903 that features a train holdup by bad cowboys, who are then chased and captured by good cowboys.

With the talkies came the singing cowboy. The first cowboy to sing in a movie was Ken Maynard, but the first actor to have a singing cowboy character created for him was John Wayne, who starred in a series of movies as Singin' Sandy. Wayne could not sing and didn't like trying, so at the end of his contract he told the producers he was an action actor and wanted action movies. They obliged him.

In Chicago, a singer on WLS named Gene Autry was selling lots of records, songbooks, and guitars through the Sears-Roebuck catalogue (WLS was owned by Sears). An ambitious young man, Autry sent letters to the West Coast, trying to get into the movies. Since he had an appeal for rural America via WLS, the Sears catalogues, and his successful records ("Silver Haired Daddy of Mine" had been a major hit), the movies decided to take a chance and offered him a singing cowboy role.

Autry quickly became a star. When he decided that Republic Pictures, the organization he worked for, was not giving him enough money, he took a walk at contract time. Republic found Leonard Slye to take his place. Slye, originally from Cincinnati, Ohio, had moved west to Los Angeles, where his sister lived, and formed a singing group, the Sons of the Pioneers, who were successful over Los Angeles radio stations. When Autry walked, the talent scouts signed Slye, who had changed his name first to Dick Weston and then to Roy Rogers.

The success of the western movies—and the singing cowboy—in America was responsible for the first national acceptance of country music. Along the way, there were some big changes—not only in the music itself, but in the social attitudes toward it, especially outside the South. Thus, it was the 1940s when "hillbilly" music became "country and western." The reason for "western" came from Hollywood and the singing cowboy.

A number of country recordings were made on the West Coast, because that's where the movie studios were. The formation of Capitol Records in late 1941—their initial string of hits included "Smoke! Smoke! Smoke! (That Cigarette)" by Tex Williams and Tex Ritter's "Jingle, Jangle, Jingle"—helped make Hollywood a major recording center for country music in the 1940s.

The look of country singers also changed. For years the uniform of stage hillbillies had been bib overalls—a remnant from the minstrel show and vaudeville days. With the popularity of western music, country performers began dressing in western regalia—cowboy boots, cowboy hats, western shirts.

The fiddle had been the lead instrument in early country music, but Gene Autry's success—especially when Sears marketed his "Roundup" guitar through their catalogue—made the guitar dominant. After Gene Autry, just about every country singer had one slung over his shoulder to strum while he sang.

The influence of the West Coast became powerful as numerous country artists went that-a-way to appear in movies. The West Coast version of country—California country—also featured pop acts performing country tunes for a wider audience. For kids growing up, all this made country stardom something to strive for. Nobody wanted to grow up to be a hillbilly, but all young boys worth their salt spent part of their boyhood wanting to be a cowboy. And part of being a cowboy was singing country and western songs.

When some of those kids grew up and became country singers, it was only natural they would dress like cowboys. And that's why so many country performers wear cowboy hats and boots.

CHAPTER 16

In a box above the chutes in the rodeo arena, called the crow's nest, stands one of the most important people in a rodeo. The announcer sets the tone for the whole affair, announcing the performers, introducing them with a few words about their background or past winnings or the horse they're riding, interpreting the sport for the spectator, announcing the scores and times for each performance, bantering with the clowns, encouraging contestants, and sometimes putting words into the mouths of the animals.

Nobody has ever done a better job announcing a rodeo than Clem McSpadden, a grandnephew of Will Rogers. Clem was born in 1925 in Bushyhead, Oklahoma, and attended Oklahoma State University and the University of Texas. He joined the Rodeo Cowboys' Association in 1947 and tried his hand at bulldogging and roping, but admits he was "never too good at it" and "discovered I couldn't beat anybody."

In addition to working with rodeos, McSpadden got into politics, serving in the Oklahoma State Senate for eighteen years, then in the U.S. House of Representatives until 1974, when he gave up his seat in Congress to run for Governor of Oklahoma. He finished first in the August 27 Democratic primary, beating opponents David Boren and David Hall, but he failed to get a majority of the votes. In a special run-off election on September 17, he lost to Boren, who went on to become Governor of Oklahoma and was later elected to the U.S. Senate.

Clem McSpadden knew the McEntires from their involvement in rodeo. Clem announced a number of rodeos where Clark competed, always announcing Clark's impressive record of world titles and letting the fans know his nickname, Ropentire.

Reba had graduated from Kiowa High School in June 1974. She had been accepted at Southeastern Oklahoma State University in Durant, about forty miles south of her home on Chockie Mountain. That summer she was out on the rodeo circuit, running some barrels and performing with the Singing McEntires whenever they found a crowd. The group—Pake, Reba, and Susie—also sang at a number of Clem's campaign appearances.

Clem always announced the National Rodeo Finals, held every year in December in Oklahoma City. Reba and her family always attended the finals, and that summer Clark planted an idea in his daughter's head. "After the finals in 1973 my daddy said, 'Why don't you get a job up here at the finals? You're always coming up here to the finals every year anyway,' " says Reba. Then her daddy suggested, "Why don't you ask Clem McSpadden if you could sing the national anthem?"

Right away, Reba followed through on Clark's idea. Clem was gracious and smiled, but was noncommittal. Then, on Wednesday evening, December 7, in the middle of the finals, he called and asked her, "You still want to do that?" Reba quickly replied yes.

"Get on over here to Oklahoma City," he said.

The National Rodeo Finals, nine days of intense rodeo competition that featured a total purse of $158,000, culminated on Saturday, December 10. The event was being taped by ABC's "Wide World of Sports" to be shown in January. Clem had been a regular on the ABC show as their rodeo expert since 1962. At that time, ABC telecast six major rodeos each year.

The first problem Reba encountered was what to wear. Her college roommate, Cindy Blackburn, had a number of western outfits, so Reba borrowed clothes from her. The rehearsals were held on Friday night, and nineteen-year-old Reba was there, fresh from her classes in Durant.

"The bandleader asked me what key I sang in," Reba recalls. "I told him, 'E.' He said, 'Oh, no, you do it in this key.' I just kinda looked at Clem, and he grinned. When I sang the national anthem the first time it was too high and it was in falsetto. Stanley Draper [from Oklahoma City's Chamber of Commerce] ran over to Clem and he said, 'Oh, this will never work.' Clem said, 'Now just slow down.' So I went back there to the bandleader and I said, 'Listen, I told you it was in *E*.' They played it, and the next night I sang before a scared Stanley Draper. It came off just fine. Stanley sure looked a lot calmer afterwards."

So did Reba, who admitted she was pretty scared herself about singing before that crowd—especially a member of that crowd she had met just before going onstage to sing.

CHAPTER *17*

Red Steagall was visiting the National Rodeo Finals in Oklahoma City in 1974. At the time, he had "Someone Cares for You" on the charts. This would rise to number seventeen and be his biggest hit until "Lone Star Beer and Bob Wills Music," which hit number eleven in 1976. In all, Steagall would have twenty-two records on the *Billboard* country singles charts, though only those two would make it to the Top Twenty.

Born in Texas, Steagall loved cowboys and rodeos. He had lived in Los Angeles, where he owned Amos Publishing Company with Jimmy Bowen, before selling the company and moving to Nashville in 1973. A talented songwriter and performer, Steagall was trying hard to establish a career in country music.

Reba met Steagall at the National Rodeo Finals on December 10. Young and impressionable, she said, "Are you *the* Red Steagall?" when Ken Lance introduced him to her.

"Yes, I'm *the* Red Steagall," he replied.

"Well, I've got to go off and sing the national anthem," she said and rushed off.

Some cowboys who were there at the time remember Reba singing the national anthem, but they were not terribly impressed. "She'd been studying voice in college," one said, "and she sounded like Barbra Streisand or somebody like that. Real high and hoity-toity. Didn't sound at all like she sings now."

After the rodeo had finished, a number of the cowboys went over to the Hilton Hotel. Walking down the hotel hallway, Steagall ran into Jackie McEntire, who asked if he was going to the Justin Boots suite. Then she asked if her daughter could come along and sing with him. He said, "Fine."

Up in the suite, Red and his guitar were performing for the group. Steagall quickly recognized the young singer as the one who had done the national anthem earlier that night, and he had been impressed by her then. As he sang some old songs, Reba sang harmony, and again he was knocked out with her voice. Reba, given a chance to perform a song all her own, did the Dolly Parton hit "Joshua."

Red was running a publishing company in Nashville at this time for Jim Halsey, who had purchased Amos Publishing. He told Jackie and Reba that he would like for her to come to Nashville to record some demos—demonstration records—of some of the company's songs. Jackie quickly said yes.

Publishing is the financial backbone of Nashville—it's really a writers' and publishers' town—and that's where the most money lies. There's a lot of country music on the radio, but a relatively small amount is purchased. There's only a handful of country music acts who consistently sell a hundred thousand copies of an album. Back in 1974 there were no country acts selling gold albums; sales of twenty to sixty thousand were more in line. Red's albums were selling about twenty-five thousand copies.

The record companies make money only when a recording is sold—they recieve no money when a song is played on the radio. The money from radio and television airplay is paid to the performance rights organizations—ASCAP, BMI, and SESAC.

This money comes from each radio and TV station, which has to pay those organizations for the right to play songs on the air. The organizations monitor the stations and distribute the money accordingly to the writers and publishers who are signed to them.

Artists, managers, producers, and others involved in the music industry soon realize the real money is in publishing. That's the best business investment, too, and as close to real security as the music business gets. A single record will last maybe twelve to sixteen weeks on the charts; an album will sell for about a year. After that, it's part of the past. But a song is good for the life of the composer, plus fifty years.

When that song gets played on the radio as an oldie, after the recording has stopped selling (even after the recording is discontinued and no longer available), the songwriters and publishers still make money. A choice oldie, like "By the Time I Get to Phoenix," "Gentle on My Mind," or "Help Me Make It Through the Night," will earn money from radio airplay year after year after year. But the artist and record company don't make a dime (unless the artist also wrote the song or published it).

Most of the creative talent in Nashville works for publishing companies, who sign writers and hire singers for demos. This is unlike Los Angeles and New York, where most of the talent comes to a label's attention through managers and attorneys.

Later, Jackie McEntire called Red and asked if her other kids —the Singing McEntires—could be part of this project. Red said no. "It wasn't a good time for groups," he remembers. "I'd heard them and they were good, but I knew it was Reba's voice that was special."

So it was arranged that Reba would be in Nashville in March, during her spring break, to record the session.

CHAPTER 18

Reba and her mom drove from Chockie to Nashville for the recording session with Red Steagall. They would stay with Red and his family at the Steagalls' farm outside Nashville.

Reba had been to Nashville before on family vacations—in fact, the only time Reba ever remembered the family traveling together besides rodeos was to go to Nashville. They had camped in Natchez Trace and gone to the Grand Ole Opry.

The drive over took about twelve hours—north from Chockie, through Kiowa and McAlester on Route 75, then up to Interstate 40 heading east, across the Arkansas border, through Little Rock and Memphis, then four more hours to hit Nashville. On the trip Jackie told Reba she was "living her dreams through her." She impressed upon her that this was her big chance and she would do everything to make those dreams come true. Reba didn't need much prompting—she was ambitious and energetic herself and rarin' to sing.

The session, held at Nuggett Studio, included a song written by Steagall and Glenn Sutton, "You're My Kind of Girl," one by Reba, "Leave My Texas Boy Alone," and two others.

At the end of the session, Red told Reba and Jackie to go on back home and just forget the whole thing. These things take awhile, and nothing might come of it even then. "In other words," says Reba, "don't call us, we'll call you."

So Jackie and Reba drove all the way back to Chockie.

Meanwhile, Red was pitching the tape all over town, playing it for record executives, whose response was generally "I don't want a female singer." But then Joe Light, who was working with Red at the publishing company at the time, took the tape over to Glenn Keener, producer and A & R man at Mercury Records, and Keener liked Reba's voice.

More important, Mercury was looking for a female singer. Each label wants a balanced roster: male singers, female singers, male groups, female groups, perhaps an instrumentalist, performing different styles of music—traditional country, pop-country, rockabilly, and the like. It just so happened that Mercury didn't have a female singer on the label and needed one.

Glenn Keener and Mercury producer Jerry Kennedy went to Chicago, Mercury's headquarters, shortly after Keener had received the tape. There they held meetings to discuss the roster and play tapes of new acts they were considering signing. Keener had tapes of two female singers and played them both; the other executives told him to pick one, and he picked Reba. "I just thought she had the most commercial voice," says Keener.

He'd also met Reba and Jackie by this time. After Keener had first expressed an interest, Steagall had called Jackie and told her and Reba to come to Nashville. There was a good rapport. "I knew she came from good people," said Keener. "They seemed like the kind of people that could handle success and you could depend on to make something happen."

People remember being surprised by Reba's talent at this time. Joe Light remembers her in the studio singing those demos; when he heard her voice coming over the speakers in the control room, he was struck by how good she was. Red Steagall and Glenn Keener had also been impressed; others would soon be hearing her and also be impressed by her talent.

On November 11, 1975, Reba signed her contract with Mercury. It was negotiated by Red Steagall, who did most of the "managing" at the time. It was all unofficial—mostly an advisory role. Red knew that first contract was just a way to get a foot in the door. It was a singles deal—calling for her to record only four songs—but the label had options for the next several years if they chose to keep her.

After the session, Reba went back to school in Durant. Then, in December, she was at the National Rodeo Finals again, singing the national anthem, before heading back home to Chockie Mountain to celebrate Christmas. It was a good Christmas for Jackie and Reba, full of anticipation for the coming years. Some of their dreams were coming true, but they had even bigger dreams ahead.

CHAPTER 19

C harlie Battles is a big, burly bear of a bulldogger—a top steer wrestler. Reba McEntire, ten years younger than Charlie Battles, knew who he was before he knew who she was.

At the rodeo in Lubbock, Texas, one night in the summer of 1975, Reba had won the barrel-racing event. The next morning, she was brushing down her horse, Silky, when Charlie rode by. "You made a good run last night," he said. "Thank you," she said, thinking to herself, "Boy, he's cute!" Just then another barrel racer walked by, and he started talking to her. Reba thought, "Well, I guess he flirts with everybody!"

Reba had had a crush on Charlie for quite a while. "He was my hero," she said. "Always. When I was in high school he was the world champion steer wrestler."

The other McEntire girls thought he was cute too, and Reba thought her older sister probably had a better chance at capturing this cowboy than she did. "Alice was a barrel racer, and I always thought Alice and Charlie would get together." She adds, "I thought he was the best-lookin' thing in the whole world. Then after I met him, we'd see each other around, and eventually it grew into a relationship."

It didn't take long. Pake and Charlie were friends—a good excuse for Charlie and Reba to get together. When you go to a lot of rodeos and see the same performers over and over, it's not hard to keep getting together. That's what happened with Charlie Battles and Reba.

Charlie's specialty was bulldogging, an event made for the big, strong, most athletic guys in rodeo. In bulldogging, a six-hundred-pound steer comes out of the chute, and two cowboys on horses come out on each side of him. The cowboy on the left of the steer is the hazer; his job is to keep the steer running straight. The cowboy on the right leans out from his horse and slides along the neck of the steer as he comes out of the saddle. He gets the steer's right horn in the crook of his right arm, then grabs the left horn with his hand and twists the steer's head until his nostrils are pointing up, causing the steer to land on his back with his feet straight up.

The idea of bulldogging, or steer wrestling, seems to have been developed by Bill Pickett, a black Texan cowboy with Indian blood. The Miller brothers' 101 Wild West Show, organized by Joseph, Zack, and George Miller, featured Pickett riding his horse, Spradley, alongside a longhorn steer. Pickett would drop out of the right side of his saddle onto the steer and wrestle him to the ground. Then Pickett would bite the steer's lip and hold it still.

The idea came to Pickett when he was an eleven-year-old boy, in 1881, when he noticed a bulldog—which was used to work cattle—hold a steer motionless by biting the animal's upper lip. Later, Pickett bit a calf's lip and found the animal stopped resisting when teeth were applied to the sensitive membranes. He used this method while branding cattle before trying it in the Wild West Show.

The 101 Ranch Wild West Show folded in 1931, marking the end of the era of Wild West shows. Significantly, Bill Pickett died the following year from injuries suffered while breaking horses. The rodeos continued, however, replacing the Wild West show as the major form of live western entertainment.

Along the way, bulldogging developed as a timed event, with

cowboys competing to see who could throw a steer fastest. But bulldoggers don't have to hold the steer still; Charlie Battles never bit a steer's lip in the rodeo ring.

Charlie Battles came from Talala, in Rogers County, up around Claremore, Oklahoma. He had married early, in 1966, when he was twenty-one. He'd joined the service and had two boys, Lance and Cody. But the marriage didn't work out. After Charlie mustered out of the service in 1969, he began rodeoing in earnest, going on down the road to whatever rodeo looked like it might let him up to the pay window. He couldn't have known that in a few years that road would lead him to a young woman named Reba McEntire.

PART 3

OUT OF A DREAM

CHAPTER *20*

Nineteen seventy-six would be a big year for Reba McEntire. On January 22 she was at Woodland Sound Studios in Nashville for her first Mercury recording session. Produced by Glenn Keener, the musicians were some of Nashville's finest studio cats: Pig Robbins, Pete Wade, Ray Edenton, Bob Moore, Buddy Harmon, Lloyd Green, Leon Rhodes, and Tommy Allsup.

The session began at 6 P.M. and lasted three hours. Reba recorded four songs: "I'm Not Your Kind of Girl," "I'll Give It to You," "A Boy Like You," and "I Don't Want to Be a One Night Stand." After the session, Reba went back to Oklahoma with her parents, who had driven her over.

On Friday, February 13, Reba's Grandpap McEntire died in Oklahoma City. During his final years, John had lived in a room with a dirt floor. Every night before he went to bed, he would sweep the floor so he could see if any rattlesnakes had come in during the night. A number of mornings when he got up, his first order of business was to find out where a rattlesnake was hiding and eliminate it. Although he died in a hospital, in his own way he died with his boots on. He was buried in the Coal-

63

gate cemetery the following Monday, carried to his final resting place by Cordis Martin, Harold Toaz, Guy Kellogg, Everett Shaw, Tod Rhyne, and Dub Wheeler.

Reba McEntire's first single, "I Don't Want to Be a One Night Stand," was released by Mercury and reached the charts in May, just as she was finishing her spring semester at Southeastern Oklahoma State. Professionally, her career was just starting to take off, and so was her personal life.

On Monday, June 21, she and Charlie Battles were married at the First Baptist Church in Stringtown.

Right after the wedding, Reba and Charlie headed out to Texas for their honeymoon, stopping in Houston at radio stations KIKK and KENR to promote the record. The disc jockeys at the stations were polite but unimpressed—another hopeful nobody trying to be a country star. Still, they played the record on the air, chatted a bit, and then Reba was on her way. From Houston, Reba and Charlie headed out to Big Springs, Texas, where Charlie was competing in a rodeo. Then they raced back to McAlester, where Reba was singing at a club on Friday and Saturday nights.

Reba and Charlie were very much in love not only with each other but with the nomadic life of rodeos and country music. They had rented a small, two-bedroom frame house from the school district—made possible by Jackie's boss, Harold Toaz. The house was pretty primitive. It cost them only ten dollars a month and "didn't have a bit of water to it," says Reba. "You had to haul every drop of water you used."

They rented that house primarily to store their "junk" (as Reba calls it)—furniture, clothes, and the like. They actually spent a good part of the summer in a Chevrolet pickup truck with a camper on the back, going from rodeo to rodeo, where Charlie competed. Reba competed in some barrel-racing events and tried to perform some as well, promoting her record everywhere she went. At most rodeos, there'd be a dance afterward, or the cowboys would gather together to party and somebody would yell out for Reba to sing. It didn't take much prompting for Reba to get up and belt out a few numbers, and she soon developed a loyal and enthusiastic—though small—following.

On September 16 Reba did her first session with producer Jerry Kennedy, who would work with her for the next seven years. On this first session, at U.S. Recording Studio, next door to the Mercury offices, she recorded three songs: "I've Waited All My Life for You," "I Was Glad to Give My Everything to You," and "(There's Nothing Like the Love) Between a Woman and a Man."

After the summer, Reba returned to Southeastern Oklahoma State to finish her degree. Always in a hurry to get on with life, Reba finished the four-year program in three and a half years, graduating on December 16, 1976, with a bachelor's degree in elementary education and a minor in music. But though she was certified to teach elementary school children, she didn't have any plans in that direction.

CHAPTER *21*

I Don't Want to Be a One Night Stand" only went up to number 88 on the country singles chart in *Billboard* and lasted five weeks. Actually, by the time Reba got married, the single had already fallen off the chart.

Mercury did not release Reba's second single, "Between a Woman and a Man," until 1977. The single made its debut in February, rose to number 86, and lasted only four weeks on the chart.

In April 1977 Reba was in Nashville for two days of recording. On April 12 she did "Right Time of the Night," "Take Your Love Away," and "Why Can't He Be You." The next day she recorded

"Invitation to the Blues," "Angel in Your Arms," and "Glad I Waited Just for You." Both sessions began at ten in the morning and were finished by one.

It took Mercury about six months to release the third single, "Glad I Waited Just for You," which made its debut in August and spent four weeks on the chart, peaking at number 88. Reba McEntire's recording career was off and crawling.

Most labels do not release an album on an artist until that artist has had a hit single—sometimes several. But in August 1977, long before Reba's first hit, Mercury released her first album, evidence the label believed in her.

Reba McEntire, whose cover features a sweetly innocent young Reba, with long red tresses and soft curls, wearing a frilly blouse, begins with the pop-flavored "Glad I Waited Just for You," followed by "One to One," a ballad of true love that soars from a quiet piano intro to a climax with prominent strings. "Angel in Your Arms" is a country version of Vivian Bell's pop hit. "I Don't Want to Be a One Night Stand" is about a woman who wants more than just sex to call it love. "I've Waited All My Life for You" extolls traditional love, while "I Was Glad to Give My Everything to You" is a song about having no regrets with a love gone wrong. The message is straight from the 1970s: individual independence is more important than anything else.

Side 2 opens with "Take Your Love Away," where the singer is gun-shy about love commitments. "Between a Woman and a Man" has a funky, bluesy feel about the joys of heterosexual affection and cohabitation. "Why Can't He Be You," which was a hit for Loretta Lynn, features a tinkling piano and lyrics about mismatched love. A walking bass and shuffle rhythm mark Roger Miller's "Invitation to the Blues," the old Ray Price classic from 1958. The album closes with "Right Time of the Night," a country version of the Jennifer Warnes hit.

At that time Reba was performing wherever she could, touring with Red Steagall and his Coleman County Cowboys. She was booked by the Lavender and Blake agency in Nashville, who were getting her some dates in small clubs.

But although her career wasn't doing much in objective terms, she was enthused, telling one reporter, "I'm so excited about it all. And Red is the one who got it all started!"

The biggest single event for Reba in 1977 was her appearance on the Grand Ole Opry on September 17. The date was significant for her family: it was on September 17, 1947, exactly thirty years earlier, that Clark McEntire had won his first big rodeo roping award. Now Reba was roping some success of her own outside the rodeo ring.

Reba admits, "I was really scared when I walked out on the stage at the Grand Ole Opry. Patsy Cline was always a favorite singer to me. I remember sitting out in the car with the tape player, singing along with her tapes." That's why she performed "Sweet Dreams" on her Opry debut, dedicating it to Patsy's memory before she sang. She didn't know that Charlie Dick, who had been Patsy Cline's husband and manager, was home listening. Later he called and told her how much he'd liked her singing "Sweet Dreams" and appreciated the dedication. "That meant a lot to me," said Reba.

Also on the Opry that night was Dolly Parton, but Reba was too excited and nervous to meet her. Reba wasn't really a celebrity yet, and she didn't quite feel at ease around those who were. She was still more comfortable with the rodeo world than she was with the country music world.

CHAPTER 22

It was almost a year between the time Reba's third single, "Glad I Waited Just for You," fell off the charts at the end of August 1977 and the time her fourth single, "Last Night, Ev'ry

Night," made its debut in early September 1978. She had better luck with "Last Night, Ev'ry Night," which managed to stay on the charts for twelve weeks and rise to number 28—about sixty points higher than she'd ever been before.

Reba recorded some duets with Jacky Ward for Mercury that were on the charts in 1978. "Three Sheets in the Wind," backed with the 1976 pop hit for England Dan and John Ford Coley, "I'd Really Love to See You Tonight," rose to number 20 on the charts and stayed around twelve weeks after its debut in May.

In an interview with a newspaper in McAlester at this time, Reba said, "Things are lookin' real fine to me, but I don't want to rush things too much." She pledged allegiance to Oklahoma, vowing never to move away. "Shoot, if the Statler Brothers can live in Virginia and be successful recording stars, I don't know why I can't stay right here."

Reba told the reporter that she and Charlie weren't planning a family for a few more years. "Right now I want to pursue my career," she said, "but in about five more years I'm sure I'll want some kids." Actually, she had become an instant mom for the summer when Charlie's sons, Cody, eight, and Lance, eleven, joined them. Though they were still living in their small rented house in Limestone Gap, just south of Kiowa, she and Charlie had their eye on a ranch in Stringtown. "I love that place and would like to buy it and fix it up for our home," said Reba.

She was learning some of the rigors of the road and noted that in San Antonio she had missed her flight home because she arrived at the airport just as the plane was taking off. "Now I always arrive at least thirty minutes early for my flights," she said.

The idea of the Singing McEntires was still with her as well. "We're workin' on an arrangement to re-form our group after Susie, who is a junior at Oklahoma State, completes her college work," she said.

Onstage she was proudly wearing her dad's national championship belt buckle for steer roping. And a few honors of her own were coming her way as her career was building. She sang the national anthem every year at the National Rodeo Finals in Oklahoma City; since that event had given her the contact with Red Steagall when she first performed there in 1974, it had become a tradition for her to go back every December.

Reba also had been named Entertainer of the Year by *Shortgrass News*, a rodeo newspaper, and was proclaimed Queen of Country Music of Oklahoma by her state senators. And she had a national fan club, albeit a small one, organized and run by George A. Wooding, Jr., in Bon Aqua, Tennessee.

A turning point in her professional life came in 1978: she was booed off the stage at the Cowtown Coliseum in Fort Worth. Reba was opening for John Conlee, whose "Rose Colored Glasses" was a big hit at the time. Ray Wylie Hubbard's band was supposed to back her up during her portion of the show. That is not unusual for a new artist; since most can't afford their own band, they depend on another act's band for backup. But Hubbard's band backed *out*. According to Reba, the band said, "Well, heck, I don't know who she is. I don't want to back her."

It was only a few minutes before she was supposed to go onstage, so Reba was scrambling. A rock 'n' roll band scheduled to open the show agreed to back her. "I ran over where they were," remembers Reba. "And I said, ' "San Antonio Rose"—you know that one?' They said, 'No, sure don't.' I said, ' "Faded Love"?' They looked kinda funny. I thought, 'Oh boy.' I said, ' "Kansas City"?' They said, 'No, don't believe we know that one.' I thought, 'I don't know what I'm gonna do.' "

What she did for her thirty minutes onstage was tell jokes, then sing "Proud Mary." Actually, she attempted to tell some jokes that fell rather flat. "While I was tellin' this joke about a duck, the crowd started hollerin', 'Get off the stage.' They wanted to hear John Conlee."

Reba walked off the stage "with my eyes level-full of tears. I was mad. I was hurt. I was embarrassed." Reba did a brief interview with a reporter, then went over to her mom, who was waiting backstage. They talked, and Reba decided, "I think what we need to do is call our bookin' agent and tell 'em that they'll never book us without Red Steagall's band or Jacky Ward's band, or I'm gonna find a band of my own."

The next week, Reba formed her first band. They would work together for about a year and a half.

CHAPTER 23

In 1979 Reba was on the charts with three different singles. "Runaway Heart" made its debut on April 21 and rose to number 36, staying on for ten weeks, while "Sweet Dreams" appeared on September 22 and rose to number 19, sticking around for twelve weeks. She also had a duet with Jacky Ward, "That Makes Two of Us," which lasted eleven weeks begining July 7, peaking at number 26.

Reba was then coming to Nashville about once a month for business. Dick Blake International was handling her bookings and management. On one visit to Nashville she stayed at the Spence Manor, a swank hotel with suites and a guitar-shaped swimming pool outside. Reba was a bit awed. "I've never stayed in such a nice place," she gushed. "I'm not used to this."

She admitted that sometimes Nashville was intimidating. "I feel like a little lost sheep sometimes," she mused. "Especially at, say, the DJ convention in October, when you've got the big parties of all the *big* artists. But I'm learnin' . . . learnin' how to be a little more relaxed, a little more cool-headed than I was at first. It will all get better . . . I hope. It has so far."

Explaining her powerful voice, she said, "I guess I got it from Daddy. He's got powerful lungs or something. He can call cattle and bust your eardrums. I got in quite a bit of cattle callin' myself."

She was proud of her rodeo roots and trumpeted that fact.

"I'm a third-generation rodeo brat," she said. "My brother ropes still, and my sister was runner-up in IRA [International Rodeo Association] barrel racing in 1971. I've just been around it all my life."

Mercury released Reba's second album, *Out of a Dream*, in September 1979. A ballad, "(I Still Long to Hold You) Now and Then," leads off, followed by "Daddy," a song Reba wrote in a pickup truck coming home from a rodeo. "I had Charlie turn on the dome light so I could write it down," she says. After she got home, her mother helped her a bit with the melody, and then, during the recording session, guitar player Chip Young suggested she shift tempo and slow it down at the end. Afterward she said, "I'm very proud of it; I can't believe I wrote it. It was my first big try at it—the first song that I would show anybody."

Next up is "Last Night, Ev'ry Night," an easy-paced song about a new lover replacing an old one, then "Make Me Feel Like a Woman Wants to Feel," another song in a moderate tempo, before the side closes with "That Makes Two of Us," a duet with Jacky Ward.

Side 2 begins with "Sweet Dreams," in which Reba sounds eerily like Patsy Cline. Reba had always been a fan of Cline's; she was nine when the singer was killed in an airplane crash in 1963, and Reba has said she "about wore her *Greatest Hits* album out." After the song was on tape and Reba and the musicians had gone into the control room to listen to the playback, "everybody got real quiet," remembers Reba. "Finally, somebody said, 'It feels like Patsy's ghost is in here!' "

"I'm a Woman"—a funky, bluesy number about a superwoman who can keep house perfectly and still lay on some terrific lovin' for her man—comes next, followed by "Rain Fallin'," a ballad about being alone on a rainy night. A stay-at-home woman waits for the fast-track man she can't nail down in "Runaway Heart." The album closes with "It's Gotta Be Love," an up-tempo number where the singer wants the real thing: if there's no forever, then there's no bedroom scene tonight.

Critics were starting to notice Reba; she had gotten a rave review from Jack Hurst, who proclaimed, "If the future belongs to talent, her share will be large."

In an interview with Neil Pond for *Music City News*, she talked about her small-town neighbors' reactions to her national celebrity. "Sometimes, after I've been on television, they strike me as funny, because they want to talk to me to tell me that they saw me on TV," she said. "But they don't exactly know how to approach me about it. They'll say, 'Reba, I saw you on TV the other night.' And I'll say, 'You did? Well, shoot, I missed it again. I never do get to see myself on TV.' And they'll just giggle, then everything's all right and back to normal.

"They're real nice to me," she added. "They don't act like I'm any better than they are, which I appreciate. I'm just Reba Battles when I'm home. And if they can't remember Battles, they just call me Reba. They want to know when my records are out; they want one, you know, and I always keep a big supply, so I can keep them supplied. They're interested, and I'm glad they're pullin' for me, but other than that, it's no big thing."

She reiterated how much she loved living in Oklahoma. "I hope I never have to live out of Oklahoma," she said. "But if I had to move to another state, it would be Texas. I thought, 'Texas is like a sister, you're always glad to see her, but Oklahoma's like a mother, that's where you want to stay.'"

She was clearly ambitious and noted that just staying inside the rodeo circle wouldn't be enough. "I don't want to stay strictly with the rodeos," she said. "It's impossible to do that. You can't hit all the branches of people that way."

CHAPTER 24

The 1980s would be the decade of Reba McEntire, so it is appropriate she would have her first big hit in 1980. "(You Lift Me) Up to Heaven" came on the charts on June 14 and reached the number 8 position, staying on the charts for fifteen weeks.

The year had begun with her single "Now and Then" entering the charts, but it only reached number 40.

After "Up to Heaven" had peaked, Mercury released "I Can See Forever in Your Eyes" in October; it rose to number 18, staying on the charts fourteen weeks—a decent follow-up, but not really the monster to get her career in high gear. If any term could describe Reba's career at this time, it would be *uneven*. She would have a hit, then follow it with one not nearly as strong.

Even if her records weren't making the impression she hoped they would, her personality was. Writer Kelly Delaney, in an article in *Country Song Roundup*, observed, "The most striking facet of Reba McEntire is not her abundant freckles or wispy, soft, reddish-blond hair. Nor is it her big-as-saucers blue eyes or the impish half-grin, half-pout on her lips. What is so stunning about her is the aura of confidence and homespun humility she casts, like an Indian-summer sun chasing away the blues of pervading winter."

Talking about her recordings, she told a reporter, "I didn't know what a recording career was. I knew there was people on the radio that sung; I just thought they were sittin' right there singin' a song with a band. I didn't know what all was goin' on. I thought they were movie stars or somethin'. If it was rodeo I'd a known what goals and aspects to look for. But the music business is so different—all I know to look for are the Country

Music Association [CMA] Awards, the female vocalist of the year, or somethin' like that."

But in another interview, some of her frustrations with the country music industry were beginning to surface. "Everything takes time," she said. "I love the recording. I'd rather record than eat, even if I am exhausted by the time we get done with a session. This is the craziest business I've ever been around. The songs that make it I never would have thought would make it.

"I think country music is gettin' out of the cornfield, which is what I want to do," she continued. "I don't want every song to be a waltz or a two-step. I think the music business is smartin' up. I mean, I don't think it's wrong for Dolly to go where she went in her career. She's doin' what she can potentially do. I don't think people are very nice to say Dolly's left country to go rock, or that she's left her roots. That girl's got talent!"

Ironically, she sometimes reflected on the end of her career at the very time it was just really beginning to take off. "I won't go on with this until I die," she said. "I know that. Daddy roped and won three championships and got him a ranch out of it. He quit in 1975. He hung up his rope and said, 'They're not gonna win back from me what I got from them.' So I'm gonna do exactly like he did. When I reach every goal that I think I can fulfill, I'll do my best, and when I feel like I'm goin' downhill, I'll go out gracefully. I don't want to be drug through the mud and have people say, 'Well, she could sing one time.' I don't want to flow along like an ol' crippled buffalo at the end of the herd. I don't want to do that. I don't want to die in the back of a bus."

Then she added, "I just hope I know when it's time to get out. I hope somebody will come up to me and say, 'Reba, it's time to get out. Go home—pickle jelly, do cannin' or somethin'.'"

She was performing with her own band, Southern Comfort, and had appeared on TV in two syndicated shows taped in Nashville: "Pop Goes the Country," hosted by Ralph Emery, and "That Nashville Music."

Reba noted, "There has been no pressure on me to move to Nashville. The folks at Mercury did ask me once when I was gonna move to Nashville, and I told 'em, 'I'm not.' They told me, 'You'll never be able to stand it, living out there on the ranch and tourin',' but I could never move to the city or move away from Oklahoma. They were worried that I couldn't get to an airport in time to fly out on tours, so I told them to make me rich enough and I'd put a strip right here on the ranch and I'd fly to the nearest airport. I'm no more than three hours away from either the Oklahoma City, Tulsa, or Dallas–Fort Worth airports, so it works pretty good."

Reba depended on her producer, Jerry Kennedy, to find songs for her. That was his job; hers was to sing the songs he found. Talking about the recording process and selecting songs, she said, "Jerry will pitch an idea to me in the studio, and if I don't like it, I'll tell him so. He doesn't want me doing anything I'd feel uncomfortable with. And the same way, if I pitch an idea to him and he doesn't like it, he'll tell me so. I'm writing a few of my own songs, and I've written a couple of religious songs lately. Jerry wants me to do a religious album pretty soon."

Out on the road, Reba had been opening shows for the Statler Brothers, another act on the Mercury label. She said, "I want to get in the big leagues and have a good sound and give people their money's worth. I want to satisfy 'em."

In July she and Jacky Ward were in Dallas to present awards to Polygram's branch distributors—one of the obligations artists have in order to stay in good graces with the label and get to know the people who work selling their records. In August she was in Casper, Wyoming, to appear at the Central Wyoming Fair and Rodeo, where Natrona County Sheriff W. A. Estes, Jr., made her an honorary deputy sheriff and presented her with a badge with her name engraved on it.

Reba's third album, *Feel the Fire*, was released in October 1980. The cover features a red-tinted close-up of Reba in soft focus. On the back is a brief liner note: "I sang this one for Charlie. Love, Reba." The album begins with her first Top Ten song, "(You Lift Me) Up to Heaven," a paean to making love with your true love. A cover of Little Anthony and the Imperials' doo-wop classic, "Tears on My Pillow," follows. The bouncy "I Don't Think Love Ought to Be That Way" is about a girl who says no in a "yes" world. The singer in "Long Distance Lover" is fed up with reaching out to touch someone with the telephone. The message is clear: absence makes the heart go wander. The haunting "If I Had My Way" closes side 1 with the theme that the singer is tired of sneaking around with another woman's man.

Side 2 begins with a beautiful ballad, "I Can See Forever in Your Eyes." Reba sings "A Poor Man's Roses (Or a Rich Man's Gold)," an old Patsy Cline number, with her Patsy voice, a smoky nightclub sound that expresses the conflict of having to choose between love with a poor man or life with a rich man.

Reba's man in "My Turn" has found all the right spots, and now she wants to return the favors. "Look at the One (Who's Been Lookin' at You)" tells the listener not to look any further than the woman standing in front of him: pick the flower in front of you instead of playing the field.

The album closes with a beautifully uplifting ballad, "Suddenly There's a Valley." Jerry Kennedy suggested the song after Reba had wanted to record "Exodus." She had been singing the movie theme to herself for a while and thought it would be good to record; but when she heard "Suddenly There's a Valley," that song seemed to fit even better.

CHAPTER 25

In June 1980 Charlie and Reba bought their dream place, a 215-acre spread in Stringtown. They would owe about $113,000 on the place, formerly owned by Lloyd and Rickie Thompson, but they planned on staying together more than long enough to finish up their mortgage payments in the year 2005. On June 25—four days after their fourth anniversary—the deed was filed and it was all official.

The ranch is situated in a beautiful valley about eight miles east of Stringtown off Route 69. Turning east onto Route 43, you cross the railroad tracks and pass the stone-crushing plant. Stringtown today is a small place, with about a thousand inhabitants, and Route 43 cuts through it in no time. As the road bends northeast you turn east onto Mt. Blanc Road. Mountains flank the two-lane blacktop. You drive about eight miles, and suddenly there's a valley, with the ranch sitting on the right. A creek winds through the idyllic setting. In front of the house is a pond and behind the house is a pasture that leads up into tree-covered hills. Reba and Charlie could walk out their front door in the morning, breath clean, fresh country air, look up into those Oklahoma hills, and not see a neighbor.

You could make a pretty good case that Oklahoma really shouldn't be a state, particularly the eastern half. The area where Reba grew up, and where she and Charlie bought their ranch, was once part of the Choctaw Nation.

In the early 1800s the Choctaw were part of the Five Civilized Tribes (along with the Cherokee, Chickasaw, Creek, and Seminole), who lived east of the Mississippi River in what is now Tennessee, Alabama, Georgia, and Mississippi. But the white man wanted this land, and in one of the most embarrassing chapters in American history, President Andrew Jackson ordered the Indians removed. He promised them a section of Indian Territory—now Oklahoma—that would always be theirs. These Indians had their own culture, schools, religion, laws, and traditions. They lived in comfortable homes, made their own clothing, farmed the soil, owned stock and slaves, and a number were wealthy even by the white man's standards. But they were Indians.

The Choctaw's treaty—called the Treaty of Dancing Rabbit Creek—is dated September 27, 1830, and provided for the relocation of this tribe to the Choctaw Nation, which included what is now Atoka and Pittsburg counties in Oklahoma. By 1833 most of the tribe had reached their new home, although thousands suffered and died on the ignominious journey, known as the Trail of Tears.

The Choctaw Nation was firmly established by the late 1840s; meanwhile, the Chickasaws had been removed by the government and joined their friends in the Choctaw Nation. The most important places of trade for both whites and Indians in this area were Doaksville (now Ft. Towson) and Boggy Depot, south of present-day Atoka. But the Choctaw Nation, and the Indian Territory it was part of, would not remain with the Indians. Whites came—military men, traders, home seekers and adventurers—and blazed trails and established homesteads.

The nineteenth century was a period of expansion for America as the country moved west, all the way to the Pacific. The Gold Rush of 1849, when gold was discovered at Sutter's Mill in California, and the Oregon Trail provide key chapters in that story.

Once people were in the West, the government had to provide mail service. Legislators decided on a southern stagecoach route that would cover 2,800 miles—from St. Louis through Indian Territory and Texas, west across New Mexico Territory and into southern California, then north to San Francisco. In September 1857 a contract was awarded to the Butterfield Overland Mail

Company stipulating semiweekly service with no one-way trip lasting more than twenty-five days.

John Butterfield was a determined, ambitious man, and a year after the contract was awarded the first mail coach made its deliveries. The stagecoaches would travel night and day, stopping only to change teams; they covered at least 112 miles a day, going about five miles an hour, despite any obstacle and in all kinds of weather.

The stagecoaches came through Atoka County as they traveled between Ft. Smith, Arkansas, and Colbert's Ferry on the Red River. The three Butterfield stations in Atoka County were at Waddell's—about three and a half miles northeast of what is now Stringtown—as well as Geary's and Boggy Depot. The stagecoach went through present-day Stringtown, entering through a gap (Grant's Gap) in the ridge above the current stone-crushing plant, about five miles from Reba and Charlie's ranch.

The Concord coaches—the kind of stagecoach you see in movies and TV shows—were used only at each end of the route. In between, the "celerity" wagon was used. That wagon had three inside seats, which could hold nine passengers. The seats could be made into a bed, and passengers usually took turns sleeping. The one-way fare from St. Louis or Memphis to San Francisco was originally $200; from San Francisco back East the charge was $100. Later, the fares were lowered to $115 each way with a charge of ten cents per mile for shorter distances. Each passenger was allowed to carry forty pounds of baggage free.

Butterfield's route was ordered stopped by Congress in March 1861, as the Civil War was beginning. Although the Butterfield Overland operated for only two and a half years, it won its place in cowboy lore as well as American history by being the first transcontinental overland mail service in America.

In 1866, just after the Civil War ended, the Five Civilized Tribes agreed to have two railroads built across Indian Territory, one from north to south and the other from east to west. By

1870 the white population began to push for construction, because the railroads would not only increase the value of land and open it up for sale and development but also provide better mail service, a way to ship cattle and cotton to northern markets, and a means for soldiers to be transported there quickly in case of trouble with the Indians. The Indians, on the whole, tended to fear what the coming of the railroads would bring.

In August 1872 the railroad had reached Limestone Creek, deep in the Limestone Gap, a dreaded place because of the deep, narrow cut through timbered hills, which provided an ideal spot for ambushes. It was here that Jesse James and his gang supposedly hung out, waiting for the trains. Although there is no concrete proof, there's a good probability the James gang spent time on Reba and Charlie's ranch land.

A post office was established in Springtown, noted for its sulfur spring, on August 17, 1874; however, a typographical error at a federal government office caused the name to be changed to Stringtown.

The completion of the Missouri, Kansas and Texas Railroad (or M.K. and T., better known as the "Flying Katy") led to the death of the stagecoach business. It also led to a great growth in Stringtown, however, which by the turn of the century had a bank, four general stores, two drugstores, a blacksmith shop, a two-story hotel, a doctor, a dentist, a railroad depot, lumber mills, a cotton gin, a barbershop, a meat market, a Masonic Lodge, and an Odd Fellows Lodge, as well as a school and five churches, two of them Negro. The rock crusher, or Southwest Stone Company, began operation about 1912.

Stringtown was a prosperous, growing town, but the boll weevil was looking for a home and found it in the cotton crops, which meant the end of that money crop for the area. With the cotton crop failures—a result of the weather as well as the boll weevil—came bank failures. Cotton fields were plowed up and planted in grain for cattle and horses, and farmers baled hay off the meadows.

In 1889 the first great "Sooner" rush occurred, with folks

lining up at the territory's border to rush into Oklahoma and claim their homesteads. In 1893 the Dawes Commission required all land to be privately owned—instead of being owned by a tribe—thus opening up the area for whites to go in and buy Indian lands directly from individuals, leading to more commingling of Indians and whites.

In 1907 President Teddy Roosevelt signed the proclamation proclaiming Oklahoma a state. On November 16 this proclamation was used for the "wedding" of Mr. Oklahoma and Miss Indian Territory in the "bonds of Statehood" at festivities held in Atoka. With hands joined, Miss Indian Territory and Mr. Oklahoma vowed a "state of perpetual partnership" with the bride consenting to "divide her vast possessions with the groom and . . . to build his wigwam with her lumber, light it with her oil and gas, and warm it with her coal."

In the 1890s southeastern Oklahoma was covered with thick pine forests, rich fields, rushing waters, hills, hollows, farms, highways, and cow trails. The pine forests had long been a source of building material, furniture, and fuel, and water-powered sawmills were operating in Atoka County before the Civil War. The railroads provided the means for Atoka County to be a commercial lumbering industry.

Stringtown was an important lumber center. The people who worked in the sawmills were nearly nomadic; a crew—consisting of about eight men operating the sawmill and another four or more to cut and haul logs by ox and mule teams—would move in and set up a temporary town that lasted as long as the sawmill operation. In the early twentieth century, sawmilling cleared much of the forests in the South and West. By the early 1930s lumbering in Atoka County had seen its better days; today the thick pine forests are mostly gone from the area.

Oddly enough, the lumbering industry played a significant role in the music industry, particularly in the development of rhythm and blues, which later became rock 'n' roll. The sawmill camps needed entertainment, and this was usually provided by itinerant

81

musicians, who most often played the piano—the preferred instrument because it was loud and a man could, in essence, be a one-man band. The center of entertainment was the "barrelhouse," so named because the bar consisted of a board set up across two barrels—hence the name "barrelhouse piano" to describe a style where the left hand plays a driving, boogie-woogie rhythm while the right hand plays chords and melodic accompaniment for the singers.

It was a hard life, and more than one man in a sawmill camp did not live to see the morning while partying during the night. But the music that survived was a loud, rhythmic, vibrant music. It fit the situation—bawdy, good-time music, made for uninhibited, tension-releasing good times. That music, mostly played by blacks, was an extension of the blues, but it was more extroverted. And when it found its ways to the cities—particularly Memphis and Chicago—it was perfect for dancing the night away. Later, these black musicians and their songs would be heard by whites, and when these whites—most notably Elvis Presley—began copying this music, playing black rhythm and blues for white audiences, the result was rock 'n' roll.

CHAPTER 26

By the end of 1982 Reba and Charlie were living the life of the two-career couple, going rapidly in two different directions. Still, they enjoyed being together when they both ended up at their Oklahoma ranch at the same time.

Reba liked being a rancher's wife, commenting, "I help Charlie out an awful lot when I'm home. I enjoy gettin' out and workin' on the place. It's a good way to change scenery. I like workin' outside because it gets tiring when you're on the road and you're concealed all the time."

"I'm always followin' Charlie around," said Reba about her ranch life. "He's either in the house with me or I'm outside with him. I try to get all my stuff done when I'm on the bus, like the expense reports and such so I won't have to do it when I get home."

"I gather up all my clothes and I do my washin'," she added. "I wash all my good clothes myself. I don't trust anybody else to do it. And I play with little Jake, Susie's baby, while she works." Reba's sister Susie was working as her secretary, in the office they had built in the garage in back of their home.

Susie had been singing harmony with Reba, but in September, when they were out in Colorado, Susie kept getting sick. "I had no idea what was wrong," said Reba. "Her husband, Paul, was off rodeoin', and I figured maybe she was worryin' about havin' to be away from him; but after she got sick on me in Colorado Springs, I sent her home to Mama, and Mama took her to the doctor." The problem? She was pregnant, "and with the diesel smoke makin' her sick, and me knowin' it wouldn't be too long before she'd be gettin' bigger and maybe havin' mornin' sickness a little more and havin' to quit anyway, she said she'd start keepin' my books for me."

Reba and Charlie were clearly in love. "We've grown together with music and rodeo ever since we've been married," she said with a smile. And she loved the ranch. "I don't ever want to leave that ranch," she said. "It was the first place Charlie and I ever bought and it's real special to me."

She also liked Stringtown because she "fits in," she said. "I am just common too. The people are really good down there. It's home. I go to church there and I buy groceries in Atoka or McAlester."

At that time they were running about six hundred head of cattle on their 215-acre spread.

Reba admitted that when she was home she liked to read romance novels—Janet Dailey was a favorite author, as well as Danielle Steel—and tend her flowers. She also said she liked Louis L'Amour's books, enjoyed painting western scenes in oil, and liked going to movies, noting that *Gone With the Wind, On Golden Pond, Coal Miner's Daughter*, and *Raiders of the Lost Ark* were favorites.

Onstage she might wear sequined blouses, stretch pants, and knee-high boots, but at home she was more likely to have "a bandana around my head, cutoffs, no makeup, and a T-shirt. That's what I usually wear offstage."

A typical day for her at the ranch was to "get up about six-thirty or seven and have my usual peanut butter and syrup sandwich with a glass of milk. Then I do my book work. From about nine to eleven I'll do some interviews, then I have to cook dinner for Charlie and the two guys who help him. If the guys don't show up that day, I'll go with Charlie to help him doctor the sick ones. After helping Charlie, I'll do some ironing and watch the soap operas. My favorite is 'All My Children,' but I also like 'One Life to Live,' 'Ryan's Hope' and 'General Hospital.'"

Reba's cooking had improved a bit from the days when dinner sometimes consisted entirely of beans. Still, she wasn't a Julia Child in the kitchen. "I like to cook when I'm not burned out on it," she said. "Charlie's real nice and understanding about my cooking. Actually, he's a better cook than I am!"

Reba added, "With me traveling around doing concerts and Charlie doing rodeos, we are only home together about two months out of each year. But we both love it out here. If we had our druthers, we'd be here the whole time." Still, she was spending less and less time at home and more on the road promoting her career.

In February she had been home three days, although "March was a real slack month for us. We didn't make any money, but we got to spend a lot of time at home." The bookings were pretty steady through the summer and fall until mid-December. She would take a break over Christmas before playing a date for New Year's Eve.

Traveling had been made easier in 1982, when Charlie had given her a big Silver Eagle bus as a Mother's Day present. Up until then she had been traveling with Susie in a Lincoln Mark

IV while the band rode in a van with a trailer hooked behind. The new bus had six bunks for her band members and a room just for Reba in the back.

Charlie sometimes traveled with her. "In the spring and fall, his cattle demand his time," said Reba. "But when his cattle are out on the grass, he goes out with me."

Someone had asked Charlie if he knew what he was getting into when he married Reba. He replied, "No, not really."

Reba quickly countered, "Oh, you knew! You knew I was going to be a country singer, you just didn't know I was going to get this far. Because the night we got married—it was Monday night, 6 P.M.—the next morning we were promoting the first single, 'I Don't Want to Be a One Night Stand.' We spent our honeymoon promoting that record in Houston."

Charlie sheepishly replied, "Oh yeah. We knew she was going to sing. We just didn't know how far she'd get."

But Charlie couldn't help her much with her music career or songwriting. "He's not musically inclined at all," said Reba, "but he tells me if something is a good idea, or if it sounds right. He's a good critic, and I really respect his judgment."

Being away so much, she missed riding horses. "I never get to ride a whole lot anymore," she said.

"I give my all to music, and fortunately, I've got a husband who's right in there with me," said Reba. "And we work real hard. We love each other very much, and we work hard on the music. If I'm on the road and he's at home, it's still music. That's what we're thinking about, although he does take care of the home place and run a bunch of cattle. The music is still in the forefront of our minds all the time."

Getting recognition was a bit frustrating for both of them. By 1982 Reba had been in the business about six years, but had not yet been nominated for a major award.

Did they ever get on each other's nerves? "Oh, yeah," said Reba. "We fight and we make up and we have a big time." Still, Reba said that show business "is strengthening our marriage. When I'm home, we make up for lost time."

Reba was living in two different worlds: the world of country music in Nashville and out on the road, and the world of rodeos and ranching in the great state of Oklahoma. And she loved both. She told one interviewer, talking over the phone while she was at home on her ranch, that as soon as the interview was finished, "I've got to run into Atoka and pick up some B-12 and some other vitamins and medicines. Charlie just got a new load of cattle today and we've got to feed them their medicine and take them down to the range at Caddo. I relax and get to rest when I'm out on the road."

Reba felt blessed. "The good Lord must love me 'cause he just keeps me going," she said. "Sometimes I don't even know how. But I get a big kick out of it. I love it, it's what I've always wanted."

CHAPTER 27

Also in June 1980—along about the same time Reba and Charlie were buying their ranch—*Urban Cowboy* appeared. The movie starred John Travolta—who had been the star of another landmark music movie, *Saturday Night Fever*, a couple of years earlier—and Deborah Winger.

The movie was based on the life of a young man in Houston who frequented Gilley's, where young workers dressed up like cowboys and gathered at night to ride the mechanical bull and live the life of a cowboy without any live horses, cows, or real dirt around. It pointed out an interesting notion that you could be a "real" cowboy even through you worked in a factory or an office somewhere in the heart of a city. All you had to do was dress cowboy, drive a pickup truck, and listen to country music.

The immediate result was a boost in sales of cowboy hats, jeans, boots, western shirts, pickup trucks, and country music for about a year or so after the movie was released. Ironically, the craze did not help Reba McEntire much. For some reason, the movie proved much more beneficial to those who *looked* like cowboys than those who *lived* like cowboys, to those who rode mechanical animals rather than those who rode real ones.

Actually, that fits a pattern. Going back to the early popularization of the West, it was Easterners like Owen Wister, Frederic Remington, Teddy Roosevelt, and Zane Grey who, because of their heightened awareness of a new environment (along with their own unique talents) would create the image of the cowboy and the West for those outside this culture. In general, it is the outsider who can see with full clarity the particular characteristics that make something unique. What the natives take for granted, the unitiated see in bold terms, a sharp contrast to what they are used to.

While there has always been some antipathy toward Easterners by Westerners, the fact remains that the whole myth of the cowboy and the West was popularized by those who were *not* in that culture or who, like Buffalo Bill Cody, carried that culture outside its native habitat. And, just as Hollywood created the singing cowboy and thus popularized western music and cowboy singers in the 1930s (as well as the cowboy shows on television in the 1950s and early 1960s), so it was Hollywood again that popularized the urban cowboy. Hollywood showed him what to look like, what to drive, and what to listen to. When it comes to popularizing cowboys and the rodeo life, imbedding the myth of the West into American consciousness, Hollywood be thy name.

The effects on real cowboys and rodeos and country music are quick but usually short-lived. First, a lot of people will see it as a fashion parade and buy all the right clothes. Next, there will be an increased attendance at rodeos and other "cowboy" events. And third, country music will sell a lot of records for a while.

Thus it was that in the big record biz crash of 1979, when sales plummeted and companies fired thousands of employees (due as much to bad business practices within the recording companies as to the economic recession itself), country music was exempted. In fact, these were boom years for country music, as it was now considered hip.

And coming out of country music came a new group of performers who dressed like—what else?—cowboys. First was Johnny Lee, the singer at Gilley's who appeared in the movie. Then George Strait, with his big white Resistol hat singing straight-ahead Texas music, a mixture of traditional country, honky-tonk, and western swing. And after Strait paved the way, a succession of new singers emerged who sang traditional country, many of them dressed like cowboys.

Meanwhile, Reba was wearing spandex pants and shiny tops. Rather than singing roots music, she was singing Nashville pop-style country numbers. The kind of music that calls itself country because the record arrives at the radio station with a Nashville postmark.

Underlying all this is a basic rite of passage: public people tend to reinvent themselves. On the one hand, the urban folk revival of the 1960s was mostly a bunch of middle-class kids dressed up to look like Okies and singing songs about working in coal mines or growing up in poverty. On the other hand, the country music performers who really had grown up poor dressed in rhinestone suits and bought Cadillacs and big homes in middle-class neighborhoods as soon as they were able.

Somehow, we all want to be what we're not. And so we invent new selves to cover our roots and present to the public the image of what we wish to be. Reba wanted to be a big star, known and loved throughout the world, not confined to her Oklahoma heritage. And so she dressed the part and, in many subtle ways, moved away from her roots at the same time she embraced them, searching for glamour when the rest of the world shunned it.

By the end of 1982, though, the world was ready for a little more glamour. The urban-cowboy craze had run its course and the people who follow fads were ready to shuck their jeans and cowboy boots and get into a tuxedo. Meanwhile, back at the ranch, the true country fans were getting restless. Some of those folks dressed up like cowboys weren't singing real country music; they had changed their clothes but not their sound. Country fans had seen a lot of cowboy hats in the past couple of years, but they were still waiting for some traditional country music to go along with the look. Fortunately, there was hope; a whole trend of new traditionalism was headed this-a-way.

CHAPTER 28

Reba's bookings had picked up with her first Top Ten hit, "Up to Heaven." "The song did a lot of good," said Reba, speaking in early 1982. "I didn't spend a lot of time on the road until last August. There was nothing scheduled for October and November. Now every week is filled."

Reba and Charlie had come to Nashville to do interviews and take care of some business and again stayed at the Spence Manor. The year before Charlie had a steer horn him in the chest. Having a husband competing in the rodeo ring tends to worry a wife; Reba was no exception.

A reporter asked Charlie to explain bulldogging, and Charlie's shyness—as well as his being a bit ill at ease talking with someone who didn't have much familiarity with rodeo—made it difficult.

"It's hard to explain," he said. "They turn a steer loose out of the chute and there's two horses on each side. The guy on the right tries to catch him and throw him down, while the other one keeps him straight."

The reporter asked if it was dangerous. "Well, if you don't know what you're doin', I guess it would be."

Reba tried to help explain. "See, you kind of lay off your horse and grab the steer around the horns, and your feet hit the ground, you try to wrassle him down," she said.

Being in rodeos is dangerous: country singer Helen Cornelius's son had recently been killed while rodeoing, and a cowboy up in Cheyenne had been permanently paralyzed when a steer he was bulldogging flipped over on him, breaking the cowboy's neck. "I don't like Charlie enterin' in Cheyenne," said Reba. "I get worried about Charlie when he's off rodeoin'. You try not to think about it but . . ."

Charlie had seen *Urban Cowboy*, but Reba hadn't. Talking about the movie, comparing real rodeo life with riding a bucking machine, Charlie said, "Actually, a lot of those boys in the picture, aside from Travolta, were really rodeo riders. Of course, they can run the controls on that thing and make it go so slow that anybody could ride it. Then they can make it so fast that nobody could ride it. Still, it doesn't ever get like ridin' a real bull."

The difference between the mechanical bull and a real one, according to Charlie, was that "a real bull's skin is so loose that even if you have a good hold on him, his hide turns on a rope." Reba chimed in, "Then, too, when you're on the mechanical bull, you know you're going to fall off into pillows or hay. But when you fall off a real bull, you've still got to worry about where that bull is. Besides, you're hitting the ground."

Still, Charlie thought the urban-cowboy fad would help rodeo and real cowboys, although with weekend cowboys, "the Association of Rodeo Cowboys wouldn't let them in anyway. It costs two hundred dollars a year to join, and you have to be a real cowboy to get into it. But the rodeo movies will help, because now the audience feels more of an identification with cowboys, and even just buying a ticket helps out."

Reba noted one thing about the urban-cowboy craze that didn't help rodeo cowboys. "It's hard for a real cowboy to find a good western shirt these days," she said. "They're in such demand. I used to think a thirty-eight-dollar shirt was expensive. Now they're going up more. When we're home, we buy them

90

in a little ol' bitty department store. Charlie would fall over dead if I ever bought him anything more than a sixteen-dollar shirt. I would myself."

Reba thought the urban-cowboy craze would last "another couple or three years. Maybe five. But I doubt it." Then, talking about John Travolta, who had helped create the disco craze with the movie *Saturday Night Fever* before leading the way in the urban-cowboy phenomena, she added, "I just hope he doesn't do something wild that we all can't stand next!"

In 1980 they had gone to a lot of rodeos—"about eighty," Reba said. "He and I and his two boys slept in the front section of his big horse trailer. We never did get a motel room." But Charlie was slowing down on the rodeo circuit and just about ready to quit.

The rodeo life had helped Charlie understand Reba's life on the road in the music business. "Charlie's rodeoed," said Reba. "So he doesn't mind my traveling. He understands the hardships as well as the good times. He's done it himself, so he understands my way of life. He also knows what I'll have to go through to get to the top. He was champion three years in a row. That means working hard and beating everyone else out. But he also knows I can't stay at the top. It's just like rodeo; there's gonna be somebody younger and better who's gonna beat you out. So graciously step aside and let them have it."

She added, "I might be sixty-five when I retire. I don't think age has anything to do with it. I think it depends on the individual, on how much class and personality they have, as well as their talent as a singer."

In 1981 she had three hit singles. In March she released "I Don't Think Love Ought to Be That Way," which rose to number thirteen; in July came "Today All Over Again," which was her second Top Ten—reaching number 5—and in November she released "Only You (And You Alone)," a pop hit for the Platters in 1955, the year she was born.

More significantly, her records were staying on the charts

longer—sixteen weeks for "I Don't Think Love Ought to Be That Way," nineteen weeks for "Today All Over Again," and eighteen weeks for "Only You."

She was staying busy and making some key media appearances in 1981. In February she had been working on a new album with Jerry Kennedy, taped an upcoming segment of "Pop Goes the Country," and guested on Ralph Emery's syndicated radio show. In October, she went to L.A. for an appearance on "The Mike Douglas Show," singing "Today All Over Again." The program was scheduled to air in November.

In August her fourth album was released. On *Heart to Heart*, Reba appears on the cover in a green dress, looking a little harsh and a little out of focus.

The album begins with the easygoing "Indelibly Blue," followed by "Ease the Fever," an up-tempo song promising to provide comfort to the singer's man. "There Ain't No Love" pledges undying loyalty; on "How Does It Feel to Be Free," Reba, with just a piano, asks what it's like being you without me around. Side 1 closes with the old Platters classic, "Only You."

Side 2 opens with "Today All Over Again," a good, solid, three-chord country ballad with Ricky Skaggs singing harmony. "Gonna Love You (Till the Cows Come Home)" is another statement of undying devotion. The up-tempo "Who?" features Reba asking who could love a man like this incredible woman. "Small Two-Bedroom Starter" is the most interesting number, a song about a house and the memories it holds. The album closes with "Love by Love," a lively song thanking the man who day-by-day leads her step-by-step to happiness.

CHAPTER *29*

Reba was determined to have a good live show; it was important for her to give folks who came to see her their money's worth. "What I'm working on is getting my band together," she told a reporter in 1981. "I've gone through two bands so far, trying to get the right sound. The ones I had before were good enough for dances and stuff, but when we're playing concerts with the Statlers, it merits a better-quality band. We've got the record company, the album, the single, and the songs. Now we need the show."

Apparently, she was making good headway. In March Tom Carter of the *Tulsa World*, reviewing her concert at the Mabee Center, observed that "Reba McEntire is destined to become country music's next female superstar. She has the vocal prowess of Patsy Cline, the natural charm of Loretta Lynn. Onstage, she is immensely composed, as evidenced by repeated microphone malfunctions that didn't faze her performance. The comparative newcomer eased through her repertoire with all the control of a diamond cutter on deadline."

Earlier in the year she had gone to Los Angeles to be advised by a choreographer. After playing a record and showing him her stage moves, "I got to asking him what I should wear onstage. He said, 'Anything that's comfortable. Never wear anything that's uncomfortable.' So I got to playing around with it, and the more I wore sequined tops, spandex britches, and knee boots, the sassier I felt and the better I performed. I felt kind of cocky."

"It's really strange how clothes affect your mood," said Reba. "When we opened some shows for Mickey Gilley and T. G. Sheppard, the first two nights I wore my stretch satin and sequined top. Then the last night I thought, 'Well, I guess every-

93

body's tired of me wearin' this.' So I wore my Wranglers and a shiny top. And the show was a fiasco. I felt underdressed. I didn't feel comfortable, up, sassy. Charlie said, 'I don't know what the difference is, but don't you ever wear anything but what you had on last night. It's like the difference between night and day. You didn't have any pizzazz at all about you tonight.'"

She was doing a lot more traveling, but commented, "It's simple to me. It's a lot simpler than playing four-hour dances for a bunch of rowdy drunks, like I've done back home. On the road, I play thirty minutes a night; I'm very well taken care of; they give you a dressing room, food to eat before the show, and it's all family entertainment. And I'm sort of used to traveling. I'm married to a rodeo cowboy, so traveling is something I know."

She had been on "The Tonight Show" with Johnny Carson, which she effused "was really excitin'. I was scared to death, of course. Johnny Carson was even there for the 'Tonight' thing. I did two songs but I didn't get to sit down and talk."

Out on the road, she'd worked with Red Steagall, Merle Haggard, the Statler Brothers, Larry Gatlin, Jacky Ward, Alabama, and B. J. Thomas.

She was also confronting the issue of being a woman in the country music business. "There's a lot of people who would give advice to females to make their way to the top a little quicker in certain sexual ways," she observed. "I've heard that since I was a kid, that you can do better faster by paying so-and-so off or by being somebody's girlfriend for a day or so. But I've never had to do any of that. I've always been around good people, and Red Steagall kept me away from the chuckholes in the business."

Red Steagall "taught me that I could get onstage and sing my songs and be a lady and not have to try to be sexy or tell dirty jokes," said Reba. "If there will ever be a way I could repay Red for what he's done for me, I'll do it, but I haven't found it yet." She knew that Red was "a horse fanatic" and said, "maybe one of these days I'll find that horse he wants." Ironically, she has never recorded a Red Steagall song on any of her albums, although it was Red's songwriting that brought her to Nashville and got her a major record deal.

"I want to be successful, definitely," said Reba. "But I want to be respected. I want everybody in the industry to like me. I'm not going to kiss anybody or pay anybody off. I'm not going to do that. I have to look at myself in the mirror in the morning."

Privately, Reba had told Charlie that "if I got a Top Ten and we got us a place, that I was gonna have a baby." Then she changed her mind and said, "I'm gonna wait just a little bit longer. It'd be tough on a kid to have one right now."

Reba was now making more money than Charlie, and she noted the change. "He was the breadwinner in the family the first four years we were married, and now it's coming on that I am," she said. "We've got a nice home, and both of us are working our tails off for it." But, she added, "I couldn't do what I'm doing without him, and he couldn't do what he's doing without me, so we're just very happy to have each other."

CHAPTER *30*

R odeos have meant a great deal to Reba McEntire. First, there was the heritage of watching her father and grandfather rodeo. Her first singing in "public" occurred during the Cheyenne Rodeo, when she was five. She loved barrel racing, in which she competed, and she met her husband at a rodeo. Indeed, a lot of their courtship took place at rodeos.

Reba did some of her first singing at rodeos with the Singing McEntires. Then, after she got her recording contract but before she had any big hits, she still went to rodeos. And at the dances afterward, one cowboy remembers, "the people would get to clapping and say, 'Let's have Reba sing.' We'd holler for her and that would get her up, and she'd sing for the cowboys after the rodeo even if she wasn't booked. Those rodeo people gave her a big boost in her early career. Back then, that's mostly who her fans were—rodeo cowboys."

The list could go on: it was her singing "The Star Spangled Banner" at the National Rodeo Finals in 1974 that brought her to the attention of Red Steagall and set in motion her being signed to Mercury Records. And rodeo gave her an identity and image. It gave her something to talk about in interviews and established her credentials as genuine country. It gave her friends, support, ambition, and her first taste of the traveling life.

Even by 1982 her bookings still contained a significant amount of appearances at rodeos. She got them not through the normal Nashville route of booking agents answering a ringing phone but through her contacts—and her parents' and husband's contacts—in the rodeo world.

And so she played the rodeos: the College Rodeo at Lubbock, Texas; the Texas Tech Rodeo; the National Finals; the Chickasha Rodeo; the Hinton Rodeo; Wyoming Rodeo; Pike's Peak or Bust Rodeo; Houston Livestock Show; Annual Ada Pro Rodeo and Dance; Frontier Days in Cheyenne. She was listed in the Professional Rodeo Cowboys' Association (PRCA) *Pro Rodeo Media Guide* as a rodeo celebrity, along with Red Steagall, Ben Johnson, Slim Pickens, and Gene Autry.

There were a lot of similarities between singing country music and riding in rodeos, Reba noted. "There is a lot to see, different people to see, and it's your living. It compares so much. And like rodeoing, you're not going to abuse the life-style if you're serious about it. We are all in this for the money and the career aspect of it. We're not there to party and destroy ourselves."

But as her singing career took off, she was spending less and less time at rodeos. "I didn't completely give it up," said Reba. "I married in 1976, so I rodeoed that year with my husband, but I began to see that singing could be a better career economically. Since I was a much better singer than I was a barrel racer, I thought it would be a wise decision on my part to sing rather than ride."

She noted that Charlie had steered her away from rodeos. "I'm not that good at it anyway," she said. "So Charlie demoted me. He keeps me away from horses and cattle. He says I might hurt 'em, but I think he's more afraid that I'm gonna get hurt. If I fall off a horse and break my arm I couldn't hold my microphone."

Reba loved the rodeo crowd. "It's a breed of people that will never be matched anywhere else," she said. "It's a part of America that's lasted a hundred and fifty years. The cowboys might get hacked off when they get beat, but if your buddy gets a flat tire somewhere down the road, whether you won or he won, you're gonna stop and help him."

She also noted that rodeo fans "are the ones I've been growing up with ever since I was a baby. They've given me a real good living in the music business, and I won't quit 'em or forget 'em. They've been too good to my family for three generations."

In an urban nation, with so many people living in cities, it is popular to think that any animal not treated as a pampered poodle is being mistreated. For these city folks, the attitude that farmers and Westerners have toward animals are anathema to the urban way of life. The urban dweller sees only civilized nature—city parks and pets, with an occasional zoo. But for those in the rural areas, nature is more violent and animals have a place in it beyond sitting in your lap while you're watching TV.

Some of these urban dwellers perpetuate the notion that the animals in rodeos are abused, and this rankled Reba. "I wish I was treated as well as the stock in the rodeo industry," she said. "They get pampered. You take an ol' stock contractor who's worked all his life to get a good buckin' horse or bull. Anybody's crazy to think that contractor is gonna mistreat that animal; that's his bread and butter. If that bull dies, he's back to square one. He pampers all the rest of his stock, because he thinks they might develop into something, too."

Reba's fifth album, *Unlimited*, was released in June 1982. It begins with "I'd Say You," a song about true love that is followed by "Everything I'll Ever Own," a ballad where she says she'd give it all for her man. "What Do You Know About Heartache" tells her man she loves him more than he loves her, and "Out of the Blue" is a 1950s-ish ballad about true love popping up out of nowhere. Side 1 closes with "Over, Under, and Around," an up-tempo number about a good girl gone after putting up with too much of a bad man.

Side 2 commences with "I'm Not That Lonely Yet," a beautiful ballad in waltz time that says this girl will go only so far. "Whoever's Watchin' " has a quasi-gospel message about someone above watching out for her below. "Old Man River (I've Come to Talk Again)," a hit for Shylo, is about a love who's like a river that keeps flowing away. "You're the First Time I've Thought About Leaving," another country waltz with a fiddle kick-off, is about temptation that almost goes too far, but it's only in the singer's mind. The album closes with "Can't Even Get the Blues," a real kicker about a man who's taken everything—even her feelings, so she can't feel sad anymore.

When Reba arrived in New York in 1982 for a special photography session, she discovered all her luggage had been lost, including the suitcase with all the brand-new clothes she had just bought to wear for the cover shots of her album. Still, though she lost her temper, she managed to gather together some clothes and cope with the adversity.

She noted at this time that her favorite pop singers were Barbra Streisand, Donna Summer, and Sheena Easton and that "I get a lot of criticism because my albums don't have a style to them. But I like everything from Kitty Wells to Barbra Streisand. And that's what I sing—everything.

"You know, I've got an attention span worse than a two-year-old," she said. "I get tired of one thing real soon. I like to record different things, and I like to record what I like. I want everybody to be happy, but you have to please yourself first."

Reba's career had been steadily climbing since she had her first Top Ten in 1980 with "Up to Heaven." In 1981 "Today All Over Again" reached number 5. Then, in 1982, "I'm Not That Lonely Yet" reached number 3, and "Can't Even Get the Blues" finally put her where she'd been aiming: at the number 1 spot on *Billboard*'s country singles chart.

PART 4

BEHIND

THE SCENES

CHAPTER *31*

In 1983 Reba McEntire had her second number-one record —"How Blue"—on the *Billboard* country charts. This was followed by another number one, "You're the First Time I've Thought About Leaving," and a Top Ten, "Why Do We Want (What We Know We Can't Have)," as her recording career began to catch fire. She would also receive her first nominations for Country Music Association awards—the Horizon and Female Vocalist of the Year honors. But this would also be a big transitional year for her in another way: she switched record labels, leaving Mercury and producer Jerry Kennedy, where she had been since she first signed to a major label in 1976, and moving over to giant MCA Records.

There was a lot of historical significance in this move: MCA Records owned Decca, which had been the label of Kitty Wells, Patsy Cline, and Loretta Lynn.

It was also a transitional year for country music. The boom years of the urban-cowboy phenomenon had gone bust, and the recession the rest of the music industry was going through hit country music hard; sales were weak and labels were struggling.

The bright spot for country music occurred on March 7, 1983, when the Nashville Network (TNN) went on the air bringing country music and country artists into people's homes. Reba had been champing at the bit to do more television and get more recognition; here was the perfect vehicle. For a pretty redhead with spunk and sass, TV could be a real blessing. And Reba was a blessing for TNN too; the channel was struggling at first to fill the hours with interesting artists, and there just aren't that many artists in country music to get folks interested seven days a week. While Reba was not an unknown by a long shot, she was not a household name either. The TV exposure on TNN came along at a critical time, providing key exposure for her.

Reba's first appearance, on March 18, 1983, came on TNN's most popular offering, "Nashville Now," the talk show hosted by Ralph Emery. At that time the show did not even have its own studio; it was broadcast from the Stagedoor Lounge in the Opryland Hotel. Appearing on the show with Reba were Narvel Felts, Lorrie Morgan, Rich Landers, and Dick Feller.

Reba appeared in a glittering jacket with spandex pants, high heels, and her rodeo belt buckle and sang "You're the First Time I've Thought About Leaving" in the first half of the show. The show closed with her singing "I'm Not That Lonely Yet."

After the first song, Ralph asked her if she still participated in rodeos. Reba replied that she didn't, because she didn't have time, and that she "missed it." Ralph commented on her sparkling jacket, and Reba talked about her clothes a bit, noting that she never wore "evening clothes." Talking about her career, she noted that "I don't feel like I'm a star yet, but I sure enjoy it."

Reba's next appearance on TNN came on April 29, 1983— just a little over a month since the network had been on the air—as a "star of the day" on "Fandango." This quiz show, hosted by Bill Anderson, had a section where contestants were asked questions that had previously been asked of a country star and, to win the grand prize, they had to give the same answers as the country star. Reba was asked what motto she lived by and replied, "When somebody knocks you down, just get up and try it again." The guest missed it.

TNN also provided Reba with her acting debut when she appeared on "I-40 Paradise" on September 20 and October 14, both in the first year for the network. Talking about her acting debut, Reba was enthused, saying, "I'd never acted in my life and it was so much fun. We finished at seven o'clock one night, and everybody was so tired. They do it every day, and I said, 'Can we start on tomorrow's show now?' They said, 'Shut up, Reba, let's go home!'"

Reba was also making trips to Los Angeles to audition for TV parts. "My agent has made some appointments for me out there to try and get some small roles on family shows like 'Love Boat' and 'Fantasy Island,'" she said. "You need roles like that for people to see your face and recognize it."

In June, during Fan Fair, her name was inducted in the Walkway of Stars at the Country Music Hall of Fame.

In September Polygram released Reba's sixth album. *Behind the Scene* has a glamorous Reba on the cover, looking at the camera with her big blues eyes and with her soft red curls up on top of her head. The back-lit head shot shows Reba as a strikingly beautiful woman with class.

The album begins with "Love Isn't Love (Till You Give It Away)," a series of one-line bits of philosophy that could fit on a bumper sticker. "Is It Really Love" wonders, Is this really love or what? "Reasons," written by Reba, is an up-tempo country number that features acoustic fiddle and dobro pickin' while the singer reels off reasons why she picked the man she did. The song came to Reba in 1981 while she was out riding her horse at her ranch in Stringtown and "I had to repeat it over and over in my mind until I got back to the house so I could write it down."

"Nickel Dreams" is a ballad about a girl who climbed to the top of the world professionally but stayed at the bottom of the barrel emotionally. Side 1 closes with "One Good Reason," a driving number about a woman who's caught her man cheating and now wants a good reason why she should stick around.

In "You Really Better Love Me After This," which opens side 2, the singer says all these sacrifices she makes better be worth it. Next is "There Ain't No Future in This," a great country ballad about the futility of keeping on with a man whose mind is on somebody else. "Why Do We Want (What We Know We Can't Have)" asks why the grass is always greener on the other side. "I Sacrificed More Than You'll Ever Lose" is a stone country ballad about a woman who stays home taking care of the home fires while her husband is out on the honky-tonk circuit starting other fires. She's holding it together while he's blowing it apart and she's done 'bout had enough. The album closes with "Pins and Needles," a song with a western swing influence complete with twin fiddles.

CHAPTER *32*

Just before the Mercury album came out, MCA Records hosted a private party on Music Row to announce they had signed Reba. With Reba at the party were her husband, Charlie, and manager Don Williams.

The contract would take effect October 1, when her Mercury contract expired. "It was about time for a move," she said at the party. "I've been with Mercury for seven years. Maybe you can stay in a place too long. There's good people at Mercury and there's good people at MCA. I just think it was time for a move."

At the time, she cited some musical differences as one reason for the move. But she stressed her commitment to country music. "There'll always be tunes now and then, like my current single, 'Why Do We Want What We Know We Can't Have,' that sounds rock 'n' roll, but it's country," said Reba. "I want to stay country. I'll always be country."

She was looking hard for commitment and acceptance. "MCA offered us the best commitment. I was looking for someone to say, 'By golly, we think you're the best and we're gonna make you a superstar.' And they said it."

Nineteen eighty-three would be her first year of heavy traveling: the number one hits had opened up bookings for her, and she would do about two hundred dates that year—her busiest year ever. The traveling was a bit easier since she'd assembled a good band and road crew to travel with her.

"You have to like each other, being out on the road all the time," she said. "I just can't travel with someone I don't like. I've got eight of the best guys around. We all like each other and we all fight for each other. Sometimes we fight among ourselves, but if an outsider would come up, we'd take up for each other.

"The one that's been with me the longest is Preacher, my road manager," she continued. "He was my drummer for five years. When I got my first band, he was with them, and he's been with me ever since. I'd say he'll be with me forever. He told me he wanted to quit the road, but after a while, I found out that he felt he wasn't a good enough drummer and was holdin' me back. You see, that's the love coming out. He cared so much for the show and for my career, he was gonna step aside."

Things were getting a little easier on the road. "A year ago I was doin' the concession inventory, the hotel and motel reservations, the road fuel, everything, just virtually everything," said Reba. "Now Preacher's takin' so much off my hands. And my sister Susie makes the hotel reservations, does the itineraries, sets up the interviews and such. It's really made a difference."

That summer she had been informed she had received her first nomination for the Female Vocalist of the Year honor by the Country Music Association as well as a nomination for the Horizon award, given to the most promising newcomer in country music. That was a boost, she noted. "Being nominated means

107

that my peers have finally accepted me. Maybe they say, 'Hmmmm, well, she's up in the Top Five for this trip.' "

And it eased the burdens of life on the road a bit. "It does get hard," she said about the constant touring. "But those nominations, you know, finally made me see some headway. If I see any progress being made in my career, I'm fine. But if it's level or backin' up, I get real disgusted."

At the CMA Awards show in October, Reba and Charlie sat in the audience and watched John Anderson carry home the Horizon award while Janie Fricke won her second consecutive Female Vocalist of the Year trophy.

CHAPTER 33

Her new contract with MCA allowed Reba and the label to agree on her producer—instead of Reba having to accept whomever the label assigned her—and both agreed on Norro Wilson for her first MCA album. Reba and Charlie had met Norro backstage at the Country Music Association awards show in October and hit it off immediately.

"Norro doesn't really talk business, he talks country," said Reba, "and he talked our kind of language. Me and Charlie instantly fell in love with him. I knew right then that he was our kind of people."

MCA was going through some changes. Longtime label head Jim Foglesong, who had made Reba her offer to join the label, left after her album with Norro had been recorded and was replaced with Jimmy Bowen, who had been head of Warner Brothers' country division before this.

Jimmy Bowen's career had begun back in Texas, where he attended West Texas State in Canyon and played stand-up bass for Buddy Knox. When Knox went over to Clovis, New Mexico, to record "Party Doll," Bowen went along and ending up singing lead on "I'm Stickin' With You." Both records became hits in 1957.

From there they went on tour with Alan Freed's rock 'n' roll shows, the first venues where black and white performers played on the same bill for audiences that attracted both blacks and whites. It was scandalous.

In 1961 he was in Los Angles working for Chancellor Records; two years later he went to work for Reprise, owned by Frank Sinatra. While there he produced "Everybody Loves Somebody" for Dean Martin, which became the singer's biggest hit. Eventually, he and Martin recorded five platinum albums, fifteen gold albums, and twenty-six hit singles. He also produced "That's Life" and "Strangers in the Night" for Frank Sinatra.

Bowen was named president of MGM Records in 1974 and, when that label was absorbed in a corporate merger, left Los Angeles for Nashville. But first he lived in Eureka Springs, Arkansas, for a year.

This was 1976—the year Reba first hit the charts—and the year of the "outlaw" movement with Tompall Glaser and Waylon Jennings leading the antiestablishment forces in Nashville. In Nashville, Bowen first produced Mel Tillis, Roy Head, and Red Steagall.

At the end of 1978 Bowen took over Elektra/Asylum's Nashville office and signed Crystal Gayle, Conway Twitty, Hank Williams, Jr., the Bellamy Brothers, and Eddy Raven. In January 1983 Bowen took over Warner Brothers after that label had absorbed Elektra. Bowen moved over to MCA Records in May 1984, about the same time *Just a Little Love* was released.

Discussing her first MCA album, Reba said, "It goes from country to waltzes to love songs to contemporary things. It's really got a little of everything on it. But it all stays in the same vein of being love songs. That's why we named it *Just a Little Love From Reba McEntire.*"

She had planned doing a video of "Just a Little Love," probably at Universal Studios in Los Angeles, to be directed by Jay Dugan, who had worked with rock acts like Billy Joel. She had not done a video previously but was anxious to try one.

The title cut, with a gospel-flavored piano intro, declares that love can help you get over the rough patches in life. "Poison Sugar" is a warning to watch out for a sweet-talking man. "I'm Gettin' Over You" is about a strong woman who gets out of the house instead of staying home and wallowing in her misery.

"You Are Always There for Me" is an ode to a dependable, loving man. "Every Second Someone Breaks a Heart," in a minor key and a fast tempo, says as bad as the news of the world is, the biggest tragedy on earth is that hearts are getting broken over love.

"Tell Me What's So Good About Goodbye" opens side 2. Reba displays her mastery of Patsy Cline's sobs and glides in a slow waltz, "He Broke Your Mem'ry Last Night." "If Only" is a ballad of regrets, full of "what if's." "Congratulations" is a bluesy, smoky lounge song about a good loser with a sore heart: you win, congratulations; I lost, so what.

The album closes with "Silver Eagle," a bluegrass number complete with fiddle and banjo about hitting that long ol' lonesome go on the singer's big bus with a lot of miles. She hides her feelings on the road—nobody knows what she's really like.

CHAPTER 34

At the beginning of 1983 Reba had said about her live show, "It's getting better. We're not stumbling around quite so much, and we're just going right into one song from another. The whole thing's flowing a lot more smoothly. We still get tickled up on stage, and it takes us a while to gain our composure, but not as much as it did six months ago, when we were still trying to get our act together."

In the late summer she had hired Allen Branton, an award-winning lighting designer, to do her staging. She was also working with choreographers and dance instructors—one in McAlester and another in Los Angeles—to polish the group's stage show. "Funny enough," she said, "what they've told me is to stand still more often. They told me I was jumping around the stage a little bit too much, so to calm down and just enjoy the show. Relax and concentrate more on eye contact and a personal relationship with the audience instead of bouncing around so much."

She had also commissioned Los Angeles designer Diana 45n, who had previously costumed Ann-Margret and Diana Ross, to create some new clothes for her stage show. Reba told her she wanted something "earthy," something "a little flashy—but not too much" and "a little sexy."

Reba described the outfit she got. "It's lace and V-necked," she said of the blouse, "and it's got little sequins and rhinestones and beaded work on it, real ruffly. Then the skirt is like a log cabin patchwork quilt cut out into a handkerchief-like hem, with beads and sequins on a few parts of the patches. When the light hits it, it's not just a flash like a whole sequined cloth, it just picks up the light. I wear rust-colored, suede, high-heel, high knee-top boots with it. And I wear my [rodeo] belt buckle, which I always wear onstage, and a brown belt. So it's Reba McEntire country: earthy, wholesome, feminine, and a little glitter."

Reba was clearly ambitious about her live show. "We want the biggest and the best show, not in volume, or lengthwise, or how many lights we're carrying or the best sound system, but in entertainment. We want every minute to be entertaining to the public, not just ten minutes out of a forty-minute show. And we want the awards."

Reba had said, "I don't want the audience to get bored. I want it to be a fast-paced thirty-five-minute show that when we walk offstage, they say, 'Man, I thought it just got started.' "

One reviewer noted the improvements as well as problems of being an opening act, saying, "McEntire's stage personality . . .

is improving with each progressing show, although she still has a considerable way to go. But then, being given a scant thirty minutes to perform in does limit one on developing a rapport."

Life on the road was definitely different from life back at home. The eating schedule was hectic at best, and Reba talked about "gettin' up in the morning and eatin' a granola bar and drinkin' a can of V-8 juice" that had to last for the day because "the next time you get to eat is after the show that night, and it's usually a baloney sandwich or tuna fish or peanut butter and syrup." At home she might have "charcoaled hamburgers, steak, baked beans, and biscuits with honey and gravy" as her stomach "gets all stretched out again." Then it would be back out on the road again, the stomach would shrink, "and I'm starving to death!"

She had opened for the Statlers at the MGM Grand Hotel in Las Vegas, which was a big thrill. "I'd never done that before," said Reba of performers in Vegas. "I got to spread my makeup out on the vanity and hang my clothes up in real closets. I didn't smell like a diesel when I went out onstage."

Reba's booking agency, ICM, was packaging her on a triple bill with Conway Twitty and either Ronnie McDowell, Johnny Rodriguez, George Strait, or the Judds.

By the end of the summer, she was saying, "This is the hardest we've ever worked on a tour, but it's going to be a lot of fun. We have thirty-five minutes a night, so we're going to get it down pat with our lighting, our movements—everything—so we can give the folks the best thirty-five minutes possible. I guess you could say this is a showcase for Reba McEntire—what she's done in the past, what she's doing now."

Reba loved touring and admitted, "I'm a people person. I travel with seven band members, three crew members, and my husband, when he can get away from the ranch. It's a pretty crowded bus, but it's the only way to travel. I like to sit up front with the guys. We watch movies and play cards and dominos and checkers. We go sightseeing a lot, take detours to see a cave or a park. We take the time to be happy."

About surviving the rigors of touring, she said, "Well, it's just a matter of keeping your mind together. You can't let it get to you. I have people around me and a spiritual feeling inside. That keeps me going, keeps my mind sane. And I've got a family that loves me, and the people who take care of me on the road are like a family. You have to be with people who care, and you have to care for yourself."

She related music biz touring to the early days of touring with rodeos. "Touring's nothing new to us," she said. "It was a way of life for us. It always was and always will be."

She had taken control of her fan club, making her Stringtown ranch the headquarters. "We have maybe a thousand members right now, and in July when we took it over, we had just over two hundred," she said. "We're real tickled about that. We send out a newsletter every month, which most artists don't do, but we wanted to do it for our fans. They're so supportive of us and they're the most loyal people in the world."

CHAPTER 35

In order to be successful in the music industry, you must first be *perceived* as being successful already. Reba had a touch of this at the 1983 CMA Awards when she was nominated for Female Vocalist of the Year and the Horizon award. Next, you must become a celebrity—your name and face must be recognizable to the American public. It involves sacrifices; you must be available for endless interviews and photo opportunities as well as events where you can be seen on the scene. Ultimately, it involves the greatest sacrifice of all: your privacy.

When you become a celebrity, you become public property. No longer are you just an individual, just "little ol' me"; you are now a public person. And the public demands access and information. All the rules of etiquette required of normal citizens—the right to be left alone, the privilege of privacy, being able to drop your guard and not have everything you say and do be scrutinized—do not necessarily apply to celebrities. If someone chooses to pursue the spotlight to become a celebrity, then that person must endure being pursued by the spotlight, which sometimes shines when a person doesn't want any light on their private life at all.

To be on top in the music industry, you must be a celebrity. You may reap the rewards, bask in the glow, and harvest the benefits, but you must also endure the loss of privacy, the constant intrusions, the frustrations of being constantly under the public microscope.

Reba chose to be a celebrity—craved it, really—because she wanted to be a success, wanted people to know the name Reba McEntire, wanted to go into a town and sell out huge concert halls, wanted to sell millions of albums, be seen on the little screen in homes all across America and be seen up on the silver screen in movie theaters coast to coast.

When you want to be a celebrity, the first thing you do is hire a publicist. The publicity firm that Reba hired is one of the best in Nashville, Network Ink, run by Liz Thiels.

Reba hired Network Ink in May 1984, before *Just a Little Love* came out. She sat down with the firm and together they developed a plan. Reba wanted to win awards; specifically, she wanted to win the CMA's Female Vocalist of the Year award. She also wanted to sell more tickets and more records. In short, she wanted to be a star. And not just any ol' twinkle, but a star of the first magnitude, burning brighter than any of the others in the heavens.

She would do whatever it took to get her there. And so, beginning in 1984, Network Ink worked hard to arrange interviews in newspapers in the towns she was playing—tour publicity—as well as exposure in country music magazines. The result: by the end of 1984 there was a huge pile of press clippings about Reba McEntire. At least every country music fan knew who she was and knew something about her. Network Ink concentrated on getting her on TV as well. Reba had done a number of appearances, particularly on the Nashville Network, by October.

There are several ingredients absolutely essential to getting this kind of exposure. First, the artist must tour constantly so that newspapers all across the country have a reason to do an article. And if you're touring, you better have a killer live show. Reba obliged by doing over two hundred concerts that year and investing time, money, and hard work into her shows.

Next, you must be available for the appearances that don't pay but that build a career. Even when Reba was not singing for her supper, she was flying somewhere to be somebody.

And finally, you need some hit recordings. She'd had two in 1983: "You're The First Time I've Thought About Leaving," which rose to number one, and "Why Do We Want (What We Know We Can't Have)." But the new album, *Just a Little Love* did not have any big, career-making hit singles. The title cut rose to number five, but "He Broke Your Mem'ry Last Night" only rose to number 15.

Still, it was enough to get her on the radio, and with her touring and constant exposure in print and TV, she made her giant leap to the fringes of stardom in 1984.

CHAPTER *36*

F or her next album, Reba and MCA agreed she would work with Harold Shedd, producer of Alabama and therefore the hottest producer in Nashville at the time. It was a familiar setup for Reba: she would come to town, sit in the producer's office, and listen as he played songs he had collected from publishers. Most were lush songs, the attempt to go pop from Nashville (which generally considers a "pop" song as something schmaltzy and filled with strings). Reba did not like the songs she heard; she wanted to get back to the fiddle and steel guitar and her roots in country.

Reba recalls sitting down one day with Bill Carter, her manager and attorney, and Harold Shedd and saying, "Y'all, I'm sick to death of strings. How much does this cost a session?" They told her, and she said, "I want fiddles and steel guitars." Harold countered with, "You don't have the songs for that."

That was Reba's point, she asserted. "I want to go back more to the country things like I grew up doing." It was then that Reba and Bill decided to go over to Jimmy Bowen's house—he was the head of MCA, her label—to talk with him about her career. Reba was blunt: she didn't like the songs she was getting. Bowen told her to go find some on her own. She asked how to do that. He told her to call publishers, make appointments, listen, and collect tapes of those she liked.

Reba also told Bowen she wanted him to produce her. Part of this was calculated—he was the head of the company, and she and Carter felt the label would be much more likely to get behind the records. But part of it was also musical—Bowen has an incredible track record producing hits and is highly respected and admired by most of the artists he works with. Bowen is the guy who doesn't take on the traditional producer's role as benevolent dictator. He wants artists to have their own say and sees himself as a facilitator.

Reba first made a tape for Bowen of some of her favorite songs. She compiled the tape from albums by Ray Price, Merle Haggard, Loretta Lynn, and Patsy Cline that were back home in Oklahoma. Bowen listened and nodded. "Where do you aim to find these kinds of songs?" he asked. Reba didn't exactly know, but she was sure going to give it a try.

Reba was looking for some good country songs. And what is a good country song? Well, according to Reba, "It's simple. It's something that would make you say, 'Boy, I wish I'd thought of that!' A real good melody; something that you'd want to grab somebody and start dancing to. And something you figure everybody in the whole world has gone through. Something they can relate to. Either a waltz or a swing, four-four or two-four time. And, oh yeah, it's got to have harmony."

Pop music was invading Nashville, and the charts and airwaves were filled with imposters calling themselves country. Reba knew what country music is, and that's what she wanted to sing. "It wouldn't hurt my feelings to be another Loretta Lynn or Tammy Wynette or Conway Twitty or Statler Brothers," said Reba. "Man, I won't get filthy rich quick, but maybe we'll stick around longer."

Reba described the process she went through looking for songs. "We call up a publisher," she said, "and I say, 'We're going to come over this afternoon and listen to some songs.' They say, 'What are you listening to?' and I say, 'Something real country, traditional, but mostly a great song.' We go down and listen, and they probably play me ten or fifteen songs. If I like any of them, they make me a tape of it. Then we keep that tape, and if there's something that knocks us out, we call them back and say, 'Please put a hold for us.' Then they don't play it for anybody else. It's ours until we tell them to take it off hold or we record it."

This has been the job of Nashville producers for years. They either make the rounds of publishers or, more likely, sit in their offices while publishers come around to play their songs for them. There was nothing really new in all this except, instead of the producer going through all this, an artist was doing it. And not just any artist, either. This artist was the determined, stubborn, spunky female Reba McEntire.

CHAPTER 37

In the 1960s Nashville became famous for the "Nashville Sound," which basically consists of a handful of the same studio musicians playing on most of the country records coming out of Nashville. These musicians are well known and respected for their "head sessions," learning and arranging a song quickly in the studio. It is economical and efficient—in one three-hour session, three or four songs are usually recorded. In the 1960s and early 1970s there was little overdubbing after the session.

One of the less heralded aspects of the Nashville Sound is the role of the producer, who assumes the commanding role in the studio. The producer is the professional—often a professional musician—who finds the songs, determines the musical direction, sets up the session, and calls the musicians. He (and it was always a "he" in the Sixties, Seventies, and most of the Eighties) would collect a number of songs from publishing companies and play them for the artist, who would learn them. There was always some interaction—artists could turn down songs they felt uncomfortable with and could always bring in songs they wanted to record or give some input in the selection. But in the end, this was really the producer's job, and he called the shots.

By 1976 there were some changes in the wind. There was the "outlaw" movement going on, which consisted essentially of two artists—Waylon Jennings and Willie Nelson—taking control of their careers and their studio recordings. They began serving as their own producers, or at least giving their producer other roles—such as technician, administrator, or arranger. In 1976 Reba was too young, unproven, and inexperienced for all that. But she would be a beneficiary of this movement in the long run as Nashville began to change.

With the traditional producer/artist arrangement, it may be argued that the producer is the true artist, and the artist is merely a singer. The producer decides the musical direction, the songs, and the singles released. At the time of Reba's first recordings, the quintessential producer was Billy Sherrill, producer of Tammy Wynette and numerous others, who wrote or selected many of the songs for his artists, and ran the sessions.

Most of the time, most artists never complained, especially if the sessions yielded hit songs that made them famous. Indeed, many recording artists are opportunists, attracted more to the lure of the spotlight and the carrot stick of stardom than to the music itself. The songs are merely a vehicle to stardom, and the sessions are a vehicle to get those songs recorded and out there to radioland. By and large, the producer is the driver of that vehicle.

Reba remembers her early Mercury sessions. She would come into town, Jerry Kennedy would say, "I think this song would be good for you," and she would record it. According to Reba, she had little input in picking songs for herself—by the time she arrived at Kennedy's office, the tapes were already screened and waiting for her to listen and learn.

There is, of course, the time element. Generally artists do not have the time—because they are out on the road performing—to solicit and sift through countless tapes in order to find ten or twelve good songs. The producer, with an office on Music Row, does have the time, and that is part of his job. For artists to do this, they have to spend a considerable amount of their time listening to countless songs, and most are simply not inclined to do that.

And so the artist often just sang; the producer did all the rest. What emerged was a handful of men with a lot of influence in what country music was released.

Most of these producers are, on the whole, very talented and well-intentioned men. Obviously, they want the same things the artists want—hit records. And they work hard for this. Jerry Kennedy, for example, was part of a very efficient, successful process. He did very well producing the early Roger Miller smashes and records by Tom T. Hall, and guiding the Statler Brothers to their success. These men were certainly not insensitive to artists—if an artist was a particularly talented writer, then the producer worked with that. A good example is Jerry Kennedy and Tom T. Hall.

If the singer hated a song or felt uncomfortable with it, it would be discarded. And it was certainly not the producer's intention to stop or thwart the growth of country music.

But the times were changing. Big business was invading country music. Nashville wasn't the small, cliquish, fun little place it used to be.

The economics of the recording industry changed, too. First, the outlaw movement was extremely popular, both with record sales and with media attention. Willie Nelson and Waylon Jennings both became superstars; their *Outlaws* album for RCA sold over a million copies—high cotton for an industry used to being thrilled at sales of 100,000 copies.

Another change was that the labels saw they could eliminate staff producers—reducing their payroll—and have a steady source of product from independent producers.

Finally, artists themselves wanted more control of their careers. Until this time, they were in no position to demand such power and control; they were—as Alfred Hitchcock referred to actors—like cattle, to be herded here and there. The need for a recording contract for a career was so important that they put up with a lot to get one and keep it. And the rewards were certainly plentiful if all went well: Cadillacs, diamond rings, big houses, and fame, glorious fame.

Reba did not begin to change with these times until late 1983, when she joined MCA. By the time she had matured as an artist to make this change, Jimmy Bowen was there to help her do it.

Jimmy Bowen raised a lot of eyebrows when he first started producing acts in Nashville, spending more money on a single album than other producers spent on three or four albums. But Bowen is quick to state, "I didn't just spend for the sake of spending. When I came here they were spending twelve to fifteen thousand dollars on albums when the competition in other styles of music was spending a hundred thousand to a hundred fifty thousand." Quality is important to him, and he noted, "If you want Reba McEntire to get a bigger share of the consumer listening audience in this country, she's got to sound as good as Whitney Houston. It's illogical to think otherwise. Many country artists can sell to audiences beyond the country listening audience, but they have to be recorded properly to stand up to the competition outside this town."

He ruffled a few feathers along the way, saying, "I don't think most of the people who controlled the Nashville music business ever cared how the music sounded, only how much it cost. I said that was wrong."

Talking about his success, Bowen has said, "I think my contribution to country music has been that I put trust in and control of the music back with the artist, where it belongs." And he was not afraid to share control with the artist. As he told Reba, it was her name in big letters on the front of the album that they bought; his name was in small print on the back.

It all meant that Reba McEntire had finally found someone—perhaps, at that time, the only person in Nashville—who would let her be all she could be, would encourage her to sing like she should, could get it all down in the studio, and had as much ambition as she did when it came to reaching a huge market.

CHAPTER 38

My Kind of Country, recorded early in 1984, marked a major turning point. Here Reba hit her stride musically, getting back to her roots. She also took the first steps toward gaining control of her career and her music. Finally she felt like she was in the driver's seat, no longer the dutiful artist who said "Yes, sir" to all the producer asked.

In the end, Reba would say, "I picked every song on the album. There's isn't a string on it besides fiddle, and there's no synthesizers.

"I had a thousand times more input on this album than I've ever had before. It's the first time I've ever sat in on mixing and mastering. Jimmy Bowen wanted me to be there. He even said, 'If you want fiddle, we'll get [fiddle virtuoso] Johnny Gimble in here and you just tell him what you want.' " There was a fiddle on nine of the album's ten cuts.

The cover of *My Kind of Country* features Reba outside in Estes Park, Colorado, with the Rockies in the background. She's wearing jeans and a vest, and an American flag is flying behind her. She looks fresh, relaxed, and open.

Merle Travis–style guitar and swing fiddle lead in "How Blue," a simple, bluesy song with overdubbed harmony vocals that would be Reba's first single from the album. "That's What He Said" is stone country—twin fiddles kick it off with their nik nik news, and the lyrics reminisce about lost love while hearing the promises of a new love. "I Want to Hear It From You" features a walking bass and crying pedal steel as the lyrics question whether love is over or not. "It's Not Over (If I'm Not Over You)" is a cry-in-your-beer jukebox lament. In "Somebody Should Leave" everyday details build an affecting picture of a marriage grown cold.

Side 2 begins with "Everything But My Heart," a pop-sounding ballad about mismatched love. "Don't You Believe Him" has a walking bass and a message not to trust a lying, two-timing man. "Before I Met You" is a humorous number about finding a white knight, while "He's Only Everything" features the fiddle and steel to sing the praises of an ordinary Joe. Finally, the album closes with "You've Got Me (Right Where You Want Me)," a barroom ballad of true love.

* * *

Reba was proud of her new album and worked hard promoting it. "I don't feel like there's very many country artists [left]," she said. "And I sure don't feel like there's many country and western artists. That's what we're trying to go back to on this new album. Matter of fact, I had to go back to an album that Ray Price did in the Fifties—he's always been my favorite—to get a couple of the songs that had that western swing or country-shuffly type of sound." (Those songs were "Don't You Believe Her" and "I Want to Hear It From You.")

She decided to record "You've Got Me (Right Where You Want Me)" after hearing Connie Smith sing it on the Opry. She learned "He's Only Everything" from a Faron Young album and "Before I Met You" from a Carl Smith disk.

"There's not a one of 'em on this album that's not an absolute favorite," Reba exclaimed.

CHAPTER 39

The 1984 Country Music Association Awards show—the eighteenth—was held on October 8. Hosted by Kenny Rogers, the show demonstrated how country music had moved away from traditional sound toward a "pop" style.

The month before the show, two major events had happened in country music. On September 6 Hall-of-Famer Ernest Tubb had died, and five days later, on September 11, Barbara Mandrell had been in a near-fatal automobile accident. She was unable to attend the awards show but reports said she was recovering well at home.

Leading the pack of CMA nominees that year was Alabama with four, while Anne Murray, Ricky Skaggs, Lee Greenwood, and the Judds all had three nominations. There were performances on the show by Ray Charles, B. J. Thomas, Exile, Bill Medley (formerly of the Righteous Brothers), Dolly Parton, Alabama, Loretta Lynn, Michael Martin Murphey, and a surprise duet by Kenny Rogers and Lionel Richie, doing "Lady."

Reba was a presenter on the show, handing out the Group of the Year award. Backstage, before the show, she was throwing a fit. Reba is known for having a temper that's likely to flare up on occasion. This time she was madder than a wet hen because of the makeup that had been applied to her. She raced to a mirror and fished around in her purse until she found a Kleenex, then began scrubbing furiously at her lips. "They're always tryin' to give me an upper lip," she said huffing, eyes blazing. "I ain't never had an upper lip, and I ain't gonna have one now."

At another time she had noted that "men ease the tension by cussing and women do it by crying. I'm good at both of 'em."

She was getting a little more accustomed to the celebrity crowd, a little more at ease among the stars. She noted that "I'm getting to where now, when we go out and meet important people, instead of being real quiet and not saying anything, I'll just be my normal self and act like I don't even know they're all that important, just to be friends with them. It's working out a lot better."

Reba sat in the audience with Charlie, mentally calculating her chances of winning. Nominated with Reba in the female vocalist category were Janie Fricke, Emmylou Harris, Barbara Mandrell, and Anne Murray. Earlier in the evening, Anne Murray, who had been having a hot year, had won Single and Album honors for "A Little Good News," so Reba figured this was Anne's year. It was also the year when the slick "countrypolitan" sound was winning: "For All the Girls I Loved Before" took home the duet award for Willie Nelson and Julio Iglesias while "Wind Beneath My Wings" was voted Top Country Song. Reba had taken a stand for traditional country. She wasn't the only one doing it: Ricky Skaggs and George Strait had shown there was a market for that music, but there certainly wasn't a mad rush to go on record with some twang.

A publicity photo of Reba during the time of her *Sweet Sixteen* album in 1989.

Reba's great-grandfather, Clark "Pap" McEntire, sits with son Carl on his lap. Son Kenneth is on the reader's left and son Robert Lee is on the reader's right in the photo. (Photo: Courtesy Clark Rhyne)

In 1971 Reba won a talent contest; the top prize was the use of a car for several weeks. Reba had no money for gas, so Clark Rhyne made her a deal: He would pay for the gas if they could use the car for a vacation. The group traveled west and is shown here on Pike's Peak. Pictured are (left to right) Clark Rhyne, his wife, Sue, and son, James Rhyne, Reba, and Debbie Boyd. (Photo: Courtesy Clark Rhyne)

Clark McEntire, Reba's father, is shown with the Championship Saddle he won capturing the National Steer Roping title in 1961. Clark also won the title in 1958. (Photo: DeVere Helfrich, National Cowboy Hall of Fame Collection)

Clark McEntire shows his championship form roping a steer in the rodeo ring. (Photo: DeVere Helfrich, National Cowboy Hall of Fame Collection)

The Kiowa Cowboy Band, formed by Clark Rhyne at Kiowa High School, was Reba's first organized group. Pictured above are the original members of the band. They are (left to right) Gary Raiburn, Kelly Rhyne, Pake McEntire, David Jones, Carol Johnston, Reba, Dianna Smith, and Roger Wills. (Photo: Courtesy Clark Rhyne)

Kiowa, Oklahoma, proudly proclaims Reba as a hometown hero with this sign at the city limits. The sign was put up after a special homecoming in 1984 to celebrate Reba winning the Country Music Association's Female Vocalist of the Year honors for the first time. (Photo: Don Cusic)

The Singing McEntires (left to right), Reba, Pake, and Susie, in a photo from around 1975. (Photo: Courtesy The Cowboy Hall of Fame)

The ranch where Reba and Charlie Battles lived from 1980 until their divorce in 1987. (Photo: Don Cusic)

Reba hosts the "Nashville Now" show, sitting in for regular host Ralph Emery. Shown above are (left to right) Emmylou Harris and Minnie Pearl, who were Reba's guests on this program. (Photo: Courtesy Jim Hagans/The Nashville Network)

"Nashville Now" host Ralph Emery had a show with the whole McEntire clan in 1986. Pictured above (left to right) are Reba's sister, Susie Luchsinger, brother Pake, Reba, and host Ralph Emery, making a point on the show. During the "call-in" segment, Mama Jackie got on the phone. (Photo: Courtesy Jim Hagans/The Nashville Network)

> *MCA Records cordially invites you
> and a guest to a very special evening
> with Reba McEntire at Carnegie Hall,
> Wednesday, October 28th, 1987.
> Show: 8pm*
>
> *Reception immediately following show
> at the Cafe Carnegie*
>
> *RSVP to Jim at (212) 841-8000*

Hear ye, hear ye! Reba's gonna play Carnegie Hall, and if you're fortunate enough to receive one of these invitations, you will be present at a historic event!

Backstage at Carnegie Hall after Reba's sold-out concert in 1987 are (left to right) writers Jim Bessman and John Milward, Reba, Jim Fitzgerald of St. Martin's Press, and writer Chet Flippo. A good time was being had by all.

Reba gets sassy onstage during a performance. (Photo: Don Cusic)

Reba shows style and class during one of her performances. (Photo: Don Cusic)

Reba was a bit disappointed as well as relieved after Anne Murray had won her awards. She could sit back and enjoy the show, although it must have been hard for Reba to really enjoy the awards process if she wasn't winning.

Then came the time for the nominations for Female Vocalist of the Year to be read. Then the sealed envelope, where one name was printed inside, was opened, and the presenter looked at the camera and announced the winner.

CHAPTER 40

Reba McEntire stood on the stage of the Opry House, holding her CMA Award for Female Vocalist of the Year, with tears welling in her eyes while the audience gave her a standing ovation. When the applause died down, she said, "I used to go to bed at night rehearsin' my acceptance speech, dreamin' of CMA Awards. When me and my mama first came to town, she told me, 'Reba, I couldn't do this, so I'm livin' my dreams through you.'" Then she held up her award. "This is for me and my mama," she said.

Jackie and Clark McEntire were sitting in the balcony of the Opry House during the awards show. Someone sitting next to the McEntires told Reba later that her mama was crying. "They said that Mama had her Kleenex out and was cryin', and Daddy kinda hit her leg, like, 'Give me a Kleenex,' you know. He was cryin', too! Heck, I thought I cried enough for everybody. But she was really moved."

Later, at the post–awards show party at the Opryland Hotel, Reba saw her mother. "I was runnin' around doin' all kinds of press and things, and they was over there at the buffet tables eatin' shrimp," said Reba. "She hugged my neck, and she said,

'Well, you finally did it.' And I said, 'No, ma'am, we did it.' So that's the way we settled that."

Reba had always acknowledged that her mother was her greatest influence, her greatest support, and the source of her talent. "People used to say that my mama could have been just as big as Patsy Cline if she'd had any breaks," she said. "But she had to work as a teacher to buy groceries while my daddy rodeoed, and she had four kids in five years. It wasn't fair. God gave her a voice and she passed it along to me."

Reflecting on her mother's life and the fact that Jackie McEntire never had the chance to have a career as a singer, Reba said, "Well, it wasn't the right time or place. She didn't have the backing, the support. She had four kids. You know, everybody thought if you were gonna take off and go be a singer, you'd be disowned from the family. You were goin' downhill and we wouldn't love you no more, and that kind of stuff. They were a real religious family, and they thought that was the wrong life for a young girl to lead. She was sixteen at the time she wanted to pursue it, and then she went on to teach school when she was seventeen, and got married when she was twenty-one, and then had four kids. So what she was, she passed it down to us kids. And supported us."

And, of course, it was Jackie who had taught the kids harmony, singing in the cars as they traveled from rodeo to rodeo. "That was the only way Mama could keep us kids from fighting," said Reba.

"Daddy never did sing. I think the kids got their volume from him. It's Mama who has the voice. It's Mama who taught us harmony. It's Mama who was always tearing us apart in the living room when we were fighting over whose harmony was whose. Boy, we were something else.

"God put me on this earth to sing. 'Basically He gave the voice first to Mama. But Mama couldn't use it, so she passed it down to us kids. So that's how it worked out."

Reba owed a lot of her success to Jackie, and she knew it. "That's why I wanted to make sure she got in the limelight," she said, "because she's the one that put up with all of us kids all the time we was rodeoin', all the time we was playin' basketball and goin' to showdeos and 4-H Club and rodeos. See, when I first got started singin', it was four kids in the back seat of a car goin' to rodeos, and Mama and Daddy up in front. We'd be fightin' and wrasslin' and stuff, and Mama would say, 'All right, let's sing "Please Mr. Custer, I Don't Wanna Go" or "Wake Up, Little Susie." ' And that'd make us kids stop fightin' and wrasslin'. Then, when we got into school, Pake, my older brother, and Susie, my little sister, and myself, you know, it'd be like Christmas programs and stuff. That was my debut of live performances, singing 'Away in a Manger' at the Christmas program when I was in the first grade. And it just continued on through high school and college. We had a little country and western band when we were in junior high. Pake sang lead. me and Susie sang harmony."

It was Jackie who had asked Red Steagall to help her kids get into the music business, and it was Jackie who had driven Reba to Nashville for that first demo session, which led to the recording contract. "When I was coming down to Nashville, Mama said, 'Reba, I never got to do this and I always wanted to. So if I push you too hard or if I insist on you doing some things that you don't want to do, it's just because I'm going to live my musical career through you.' And I thought, 'Well, all right!' So that's always given me that extra push when I'm tired or I'm homesick, and it's been a big help to me."

Remembering that first trip to Nashville, Reba stated that her mother "encouraged—she didn't push. She said, 'We don't have to do this if you don't want to. We'll go home.' I remember her saying that. 'But,' she'd say, 'you think about it. You're throwin' away a big opportunity if you don't wanna do it. But if you don't wanna do it, we'll go home.' And we were halfway to Nashville. She could tell I didn't like nothin' about this idea."

Jackie countered, "She loved the singing part. But you walk in some place where nobody knows you and you don't know anyone, and you get to dreadin' it."

Reba then chimed in, "I was dreadin' the fire out of it. I didn't know anybody. I just didn't know anything about the music business—none of us did. We just sang all our life—that's all we knew. But now I love it. I know everybody, and we're learnin' new things—lots of friends. I had my rodeo family, and I'd left my rodeo family to go to my singin' family. And I didn't know anybody—I thought it was gonna be cutthroat back stabbin'—but it didn't turn out like that."

Jackie McEntire also gave Reba a rich heritage as a woman as well as a singer. "My mama is a very independent type of person," said Reba. "When she was raisin' four children, Daddy was off rodeoin', but then he'd come in and take care of an eight-thou-sand-acre ranch. His daddy was there to help him, and he had one hired hand, but the four kids were just about as much help as that table settin' over there, until we got old enough to learn and keep on tryin'.

"Alice, the oldest, was five years old when Susie, the youngest one, was born. So to have four kids in that short a period of time, you have to be a tough woman. And to keep us all in line while Daddy was gone took some doin'. But Mama really was —and still is—a very independent type of person. I don't think you'll ever meet another person like her. She's not the type of person that anybody could dictate anything to her."

Reba admitted that she received a lot of her independent streak from her mother. "She was the one to really instill that in us, to say that you can do whatever you want to do. And when I tried basketball and rodeoin', she'd let me do it, and she'd take me. She knew I was growin' up, and I was bein' a kid. And she didn't push me until it all fell into place, kinda like she knew it would someday fall into place when I was mature enough to handle it."

In fact, Reba shared her mother's dream of singing country music in a slightly different way. "I thought that was what I wanted too," she reminisced. "I was just a kid from the sticks of Oklahoma who jumped at the chance to wear all those flashy clothes. . . . I was young and didn't take it seriously enough. I just wanted people to know Reba McEntire."

Reba thought about her mother even when she turned down a movie script. "I read it knowing that Mama would read it," said Reba. "It was too risqué. It was just filthy! Everybody wondered why I turned it down, but the one thing I always come back to is, 'How would Mama feel if I did this?'"

Reba said that her mother "never was like a pushy stage mother," but Jackie McEntire, talking about her kids, countered, "Did I push and shove? You bet. But I didn't make 'em do anything they didn't want to do."

CHAPTER 41

Winning the CMA Award gave Reba a large shot of enthusiasm; she had a little more spunk and a little more nerve, which came from the confidence of taking a chance and being proved right.

At the post-awards news conference immediately after the show, Reba said that for the next step in her career, "we're just gonna work real hard for Entertainer of the Year. Why stop now?"

A few days after the awards she said, "I don't know why they did, but I'm sure glad they nominated me and elected me! I sure ain't gonna give it back. Anybody who can be in the music business and say they don't want to win an award has no ambition or drive. If you're gonna play ball, you want to win a game; then you want to win the championship. You gotta have competition—that's what keeps you going. It's healthy—I love it. I don't just sing to be singing."

Winning brought immediate rewards. Reba told Alanna Nash, "Just winning has made me more well-known. I'm an overnight success, after playing in clubs since I was thirteen! Now people act like I'm a star, but I don't feel any different than I did two years ago. The differences are that I'm a lot busier, I have more confidence in myself, we're working harder, and my team is stronger."

She observed, "Shoot, I used to go shopping in Nashville and nobody ever noticed me. Now they stop me for my autograph. Even in places like Jackson, Mississippi, and Scottsdale, Arizona, they recognize me and stop to talk to me. The best feeling of all was when, right after the CMA Awards, I started getting bookings for October 1985! I'd never been booked six months in advance before, much less a whole year! To get booked a year in advance was a sign that I had accomplished something. The recognition has grown, and it's done a lot of good."

Reba knew the importance of awards and said, "They're very important to me because it's political, and that's what this business is—real political. With the fans, that's another story. You have to work a different ball game on that. But in the industry it's very political, and you've got to kind of like run for office. You've got to politick and be friendly. But the best part about the business I'm in is I like it and I like the people who are in the industry. So politickin' is a lot of fun."

She told another reporter, "I feel like we've just scratched the surface. There's a lot more we want to do. One thing about me is I'm never satisfied, but I'm real pleased with what we've done so far." She added, "The CMA to me is very important. It's my peers, it's people I'm working with and for. They voted me CMA Female Vocalist of the Year. That's a lot of pressure. I accept it. I just really don't know if I was good enough yet to say that I am the Female Vocalist of the Year. I know so many more things I want to do that I haven't achieved yet."

To another reporter she said, "I'm real happy. I said *happy*, not satisfied. In a way that's good and in a way that's bad. I'm always wanting to improve; if I have a number one record, I want another. Now that I've been voted CMA Female Vocalist of the Year, I want to win it again, and Duo of the Year and Entertainer of the Year. I'm sorta greedy."

Reba had always measured success in terms of who would

pay to see her and noted, "You're only worth as many tickets as you can sell, so you have to grow. You have to want more, because that makes you try harder. It does me, anyway."

She admitted she was surprised. "I was getting kinda discouraged. I was wonderin' what I was doing wrong," adding, "that's another reason I changed my way of thinkin' and went so country. Things weren't working out by going contemporary. I was just another fish in the pond. I had to do something different."

She was feisty from the victory and told writer Kip Kirby, "Country music's gotten awfully diluted these days. I'd like to see the CMA Awards go back next year to being more country. There was just too much pop on the show this year. I sure would like to have seen Conway Twitty and Hank Williams, Jr., as guest artists. I'd love to have seen Merle Haggard. I was thrilled to death to see Waylon Jennings."

She admitted that "I'm gonna be doing some politickin'. I'd like to see country stay country, and not have to have all those strings and horns and stuff to get played on the radio."

Speaking about crossover artists, she told another reporter, "What they're doing is fine and they're a big success, and their crowds are good, and their fans evidently love 'em to pieces. What they're doing is fine to me, except it ain't country. I'd like to see more country people being represented in country."

At another time, speaking about pop artists coming over to the country market, she said it "really hacks me off. It's like, 'Well rock 'n' roll doesn't want us anymore, we can make it in country. Anybody can.'"

She expounded further. "It's hard, it's tough. It really aggravates me when people do come over and get a big burst of success or a big amount of airplay taken away from real country artists, who are working their butts off to satisfy the public and being honest and truthful. A person who's going crossover won't say that I'm staying on my territory. I feel like I'm not intruding on theirs and they shouldn't intrude on mine. But it's a free country and they can do anything they want to."

She told columnist Jack Hurst that she identifies with Loretta

Lynn "because Loretta's been laughed at for talking hokey and being hokey and country. Her footsteps are the ones I want to walk in—not to do *exactly* what she's done, because she's Loretta and you can't *be* her, but I want to be country, and Loretta's definitely country. I don't want to go crossover, I don't want to be rock 'n' roll, I just want to stay country."

Something else about Loretta also appealed to Reba. "Her personality has always intrigued me," said Reba. "She's always so nice to everybody. I don't care if she's dog tired, whether she has a headache, is feeling bad, or what, she'll always have time to speak. I've always said I'll have time to speak. There's not enough time in this world to be rude, and I've learned from her."

CHAPTER 42

The release of *My Kind of Country* in November 1984 gave Reba another chance to voice her opinions on the state of country music. She admitted that she always "wanted to go country for all these years, but they always said it wasn't where the money was, or something."

Back on the road performing at the end of the year, she was interviewed by writer Michael Bane in Jacksonville, Florida, at a Howard Johnson's where she was staying while performing.

"They knew that I was going to be what I was," said Reba, "and that if I wanted to improve, it would be with time, not an overnight changeover, because I was just an old kid from the sticks, and that's the way I am today—a kid from the sticks. And I don't think I need to change that."

She admitted that when putting together her album, country songs were hard to find, and "we've been lookin' and hollerin' and screamin' and beggin' for 'em, too." She admitted that "the money is in crossover. But I kinda figured, you're talking to me, you know I'm country. I got country roots, country background; I live in the country and I don't particularly want to go rock 'n' roll. I just think it would be better to go country. There's not going to be many people left, especially female singers, for the country audience."

Writer Robert Oermann observed, "It was only when she stopped trying to play by everybody else's rules and started doing what she does best that she realized her fondest dream."

"Let's put it this way," she said to Oermann in an interview, "I've sorta taken my career into control myself. I don't want to be a puppet anymore. See, I didn't know absolutely anything when I came to Nashville. Everything was done for me, and I figured that's the way it was supposed to be.

"It was like a Cinderella story. I didn't beat the bushes, didn't come to Nashville and beg or demand or nothin'. It just happened. It just scared me to death. I didn't know anybody: 'nobody-loves-me-everybody-hates-me.' I was just so insecure. And I stayed that way up until about 1981 or '82. I didn't know what the music business was like. All I'd ever been associated with was ranchin' and rodeoin'."

She remembered the second time she appeared on the Grand Ole Opry and received a standing ovation and did an encore. "That's when I thought, 'There's no way I can go back now.' "

She admitted, "There were lots of times when I would get aggravated and disgusted, still out of money and still overdrawn. Once after everything screwed up at a show, I got back in the van and said, 'Oh, that just makes me so mad I can hardly stand it.' And my cousin said, 'Why don't you quit?' I said, 'That's the stupidest thing I've ever heard in my life. I'll never quit.' And it just dawned on me then, 'Well, Reba, quit gripin', quit bitchin', and go do it. You know you want to.' "

She confessed, "I attributed a lot of what happened to brainwash, and to somebody trying to make you what you aren't. I couldn't 'build' behind all that falseness. What I needed to build was self-confidence. For the longest time I thought, 'They're lookin' at the sequins; they're not lookin' at me.' Then I realized that they really liked what I was doing. It was like, 'Well, aren't you supposed to dress up when you go to town?' You're supposed to look different onstage, right?"

To another interviewer she intimated, "Making this drastic change from contemporary music to the more traditional country, well, it could have been a big, bad, major boo-boo. Everybody thought they were doin' the right thing with me, cuttin' the contemporary stuff, because I do have a big range in my vocals. But just because you've got a wide vocal range, that's no reason to go singin' somethin' you're not comfortable with."

The move to traditional country was based on a personal feeling that went back to the roots of her raising. "I'm an honest person, and when I'm doin' country music I feel like I'm bein' honest with those people out there," said Reba. "When I say I don't want a lot of backup singers or anything but a fiddle—instead of a violin—on my records, that's exactly how I want it! That's what I like so much about Jimmy Bowen. He wants your records to be almost like your stage show. He sets it up so that when you're facing the speakers at home, the steel guitar's on the left and the piano's on the right. So when the people leave my show and go home and put on my records, it's not such a big difference, like 'That was the girl I just got through hearin'?' It's a lot better. They can get it all together."

Discussing the album's songs, she said that picking her own music "was a big gamble to take, 'cause I didn't know if the people would really like to hear me sing straight-ahead country or not. I didn't know if they'd buy it. Thank God they did."

And if they hadn't? "I don't know," mused Reba. "I take every day pretty much one at a time, and pray a lot, so I don't know what would have happened."

Discussing the album's traditional sound, Reba said, "That's what I grew up listening to, and I went back to it because I wanted to be more honest with myself and my fans. I'm not contemporary, I'm not rock 'n' roll: I'm country. Back when I began recording, the best songs we got were contemporary, crossover-type stuff. If I did get a real hard-core country song, I definitely cut it. That's what I was waiting for. Now they're comin' around to writin' more country songs. When I recorded *My Kind of Country* I had to use six old songs to get the sound I wanted.

"I like what country music used to be," said Reba. "I like the music I grew up with in Oklahoma, singers like Ray Price and Merle Haggard."

She admitted, "I didn't copy anyone's style, I took bits and pieces from everybody."

Discussing the trend to traditionalism, she said, "I don't know why that is, or even if there really is a swing back toward the traditional. All I can say is I'll sure be goin' more traditional, and it's not because I'm the next Waylon Jennings, or that I'm trying to be a renegade, or anything, really, other than the fact that it's what I feel the best with. Besides, it's different, so why not?"

But she also admitted there was a price to pay when you win a major award like this. "People have a right to demand more from you if you charge them more. And you're only worth how many tickets you can sell, how many seats you can fill, how many records you can get people to buy. It would be ridiculous for me to try to headline my own shows right now."

When all was said and done, Reba concluded, "I'm secure about what a lot of other country artists are insecure about, and that's being country."

CHAPTER 43

Reba's home folks were proud of her success and, to show her just how proud, they held a special Reba McEntire Day at Kiowa High School at the end of October 1984. Some old friends remembered the young Reba. Carolyn Clifton remembered when Reba would come over and play with Marilyn, Carolyn's younger sister. "Reba was a tomboy," she said. "She reminded me of Lucille Ball—a real cutup." And Carol Johnston remembered, "She was lots of fun. I remember when we went to buy our band uniforms, they were too short for her. She wanted the long ones."

Pake McEntire and the Limestone Gap Band, a group that also had its beginnings in Clark Rhyne's music class, played for about thirty minutes. Pake served as master of ceremonies, introducing Glenn and Jan Keener, who had come over from Paris, Texas, and Harold and Louie Williams, who had come from England.

The town took the opportunity to honor others who had achieved success in the area. Bill Hensley, a local teacher, had been the top calf roper in the International Rodeo Association in 1961 and 1967. Clark Rhyne was given a plaque by his former music students. Filled with joy, he remarked, "I just thank the Lord I am so blessed." By this time, Clark had become a Christian and was no longer playing in honky-tonks; from the beginning of 1984 onward, he would play only in churches or for gospel events.

"Kiowa Don" Smith, Reba's first cousin and the IRA's calf-roping and "all around" champion in 1973 and 1974, was honored, as was John McEntire, who was represented at the event by his brother, Kenno. State Senator Gene Stipe, who presented the award, remarked that John "got more cowboys into the Hall of Fame than anybody else," adding that he was a "lifetime cowboy whose personality spread through the western half of America."

Clark and Jacqueline McEntire were also honored, although Jackie's award came as a surprise and was not mentioned on the program. Clem McSpadden presented Clark his award, saying, "Heroes are cowboys, and Clark stands out as the greatest. He is one of the best steer ropers I ever saw." After some more remarks, Clem sat down and Clark stood up and said, "Clem said more'n I could say till daylight in the morning." The crowd—over five hundred were there—gave him a standing ovation.

Reba was given her award, a plaque "in recognition of past, present, and future achievements from the citizens of Kiowa," by Kiowa Mayor Joe Longoria. Reba had tears in her eyes when she spoke. "I wasn't prepared for this," she said. "I was just sitting back having a good time. I do this all the time, just bawlin' and squallin'."

The audience stood and applauded before Reba continued. "I'm just real sentimental," she said as she dried her eyes with a white kerchief. "This gym is the first place I sang 'Away in a Manger' at Christmas when I was in the first grade. These people here I've idolized and loved. You'll never know what this means to me, sharing your life with me like this."

About fifteen hundred dollars was raised at the program. Clark Rhyne, Pake, and some others began contacting billboard companies to build a sign honoring Reba and others, to be placed outside Kiowa. That billboard was built and stands today just outside Kiowa for all to see.

In early December *Billboard* writer Ed Morris reviewed Reba's show at the Executive Inn in Paducah, Kentucky:

> Reba McEntire is too young and, thus, too much a beneficiary of interstate highways and television to have built her art from that desperate energy of isolation that drove such predecessors as Loretta Lynn and Dolly Parton. Lacking the cloistered impulse to overcompensate and self-burlesque, the former rodeo brat has emerged as both more innocent and more wise than the older embattled queens of country music. She is at ease with herself, at one with her songs and old-fashioned only in still being awed by the urgings of the heart. The level of cultural homogenization being as high as it is, McEntire no doubt represents the last generation of authentic hillbillies.

She had made some changes throughout the year, dropping longtime manager Don Williams and taking attorney Bill Carter as a manager-attorney. But her closest advisor and confident was her husband, Charlie.

At the end of 1984 she said, "Charlie's the only person in this world who's ever fought for me. In the past there's been so many husband/managers that are just total butt-holes. Charlie's not like that. He just sits back and evaluates. 'Cause I'm gullible. You can tell me my hair'd turned purple and I'm gonna sit there and believe you till I go look in the mirror. But Charlie will take in all the hype and sift through it for the truth. So when we get alone together and I say, 'Gollleeee, did you see my hair turn purple?' he'll say, 'Now, Reba, it wasn't purple anytime.' It really helps to have somebody you love and trust there, gettin' the truth."

CHAPTER 44

At the National Rodeo Hall of Fame in Oklahoma City there are glass display cases on the walls featuring some of the great rodeo performers. In the cases are championship saddles, spurs, trophies, and belt buckles, as well as personal items such as boots, ropes, pictures, hats, watches, and the badges with the entry number the cowboy has pinned to his back.

In those cases are displays from the likes of rodeo greats such as Tom Nesmith, Buck Rutherford, Jim Eskew, Jr., Louis Brooks, Edward Bowman, Mike Hastings, Lee Robinson, Ike Rude, Doff Aber, Paddy Ryan, Oral Zumwalt, Eddie Curtis, Fritz Traum, Kit Fletcher, Clyde Burk, Pete Knight, Harry Tompkins, Johnnie Schneider, Earl Thode, Herman Linder, Smoky Snyder, Jim Shoulders, Homer Pettigrew, Bill Pickett, Casey Tibbs, Bob Crosby, and Dean Oliver.

There are two walls lined with the oil portraits of some of the great All-Around Cowboys, like Tom Ferguson (who won that title in 1974, 1975, and 1977, the years Reba competed in rodeos), Larry Mahan, Dean Oliver, Casey Tibbs (who won in 1955, the year Reba was born), Jim Shoulders, and Everett Shaw, the cowboy who had goaded little Pake McEntire into singing "Hound Dog" at the Frontier Hotel in Cheyenne back in 1960.

There are also cases showing the origins of rodeo, the promoters and contractors like C. B. Irwin, Tex Austin, Eddy McCarty, and Verne Elliott in addition to displays on the trick riders and ropers like Leonard Stroud, Sam Garrett, and Chester Byers.

Just before you enter the section with the display cases for the Rodeo Hall of Fame, right after passing through Founders' Hall, is a large wooden plaque with names engraved on brass plates. These are the inductees of the National Rodeo Hall of Fame. The first name is that of Paul Carney of Colorado, who was inducted when the Rodeo Hall of Fame began in 1961—coincidentally, the same year the Country Music Hall of Fame began. (Both were modeled after the Baseball Hall of Fame in Cooperstown, New York.)

On Sunday evening, December 9, 1984, the name John McEntire was added to that list of inductees. The McEntire family was there, and they were clearly excited. Reba was proud of her association with rodeos, proud of her family, and especially proud of her grandpap.

"Rodeos paid for the ranch," she said. "My grandfather was the world champion steer roper in '34. My father won the same title in '57, '58, and '61. Pake just got through winning the steer roping at Pendleton, Oregon. That's a big rodeo. Grandpap roped there, and my daddy was just inducted into the Hall of Fame there.

"I'm very proud of my heritage and where I grew up. I'm out in the sticks, still, just four miles east of Stringtown, Oklahoma, where the population is five hundred. That's what I like. I like the simple life, the country, the fact that I'm from ranchin' people. I like the fact that I've gotten up in the morning before daylight and gathered cattle until after nightfall. All that gave me a sense of pride. I'm very proud to be an Oklahoman and a rancher's daughter, a rancher's wife, and part of the rodeo family."

At the induction awards, Reba, Pake, and Susie reunited as the Singing McEntires to sing "The Ballad of John McEntire." Reba, Pake, and Susie exchanged stanzas, accompanied by Clark Rhyne on fiddle while Pake played guitar. At the ceremony, Reba said of her grandpap, "He was always very special to us. He always had a twinkle in his eye, a smile, and a laugh. He always laughed a lot and cracked a lot of jokes, especially practical jokes, as a lot of you probably saw firsthand. He was a picturesque grand-pappy. And I wish so much that my little boys could have known him, because he was such a man and we loved him so much."

A couple of chapters closed for Reba McEntire in 1984. In December she performed the national anthem at the National Rodeo Finals for the last time. After this, the event would move from Oklahoma City to Las Vegas. But she would get her own big rodeo buckle out of this, to commemorate the ten years she had sung the national anthem at the finals.

This was also the year Charlie Battles retired from the rodeo ring. For the past several years he had been cutting back significantly on the number of events he had been entering.

After the Rodeo Hall of Fame induction and the National Rodeo Finals, Reba performed at Billy Bob's, the big dance club in Fort Worth, then took a short Christmas break before concluding the year with a New Year's Eve concert with Mel Tillis in Tulsa.

While at Billy Bob's she told a reporter, "I'd like to draw larger crowds, to have two buses on tour, our own sound and lighting engineers, and I'd like to win the Music City News Award because that's voted on by the fans."

PART 5

THE MISTRESS

OF MELANCHOLY

CHAPTER 45

On June 10, 1985, Reba won the Top Female Vocalist award at the nineteenth annual Music City News Awards. The month before, on May 7, she had won the Academy of Country Music's Top Female Vocalist award. Also in May she had been the female vocalist named a member of the TNN Winners Circle in that network's award ceremony.

These awards joined the CMA Female Vocalist of the Year award at Reba's home in Oklahoma. The CMA trophy was "sittin' in there on the mantel of our fireplace," she said. "I don't let many people pick it up, but I'll sure show it to 'em. Lee Greenwood said he broke his last year, chipped it. So I don't want that to happen to mine."

The awards were important to her, she said. "You know, it don't mean something to some people, just like holidays don't mean something to some people. Award shows do mean a lot to me; like I said the night I won the award, I'd been watching them since Merle Haggard was winning for 'Okie From Muskogee.' It's something that you just dream about, like winning a championship rodeo. It's something you dream about doin'. And

143

to finally accomplish it before I'm thirty years old, that's a big highlight of my life."

The one big award she had not captured was a Grammy, although she had been a presenter on that show in February. While there, she suffered some humiliation from rock star Sting. "I went up to him and stuck out my hand and introduced myself," Reba told reporter Bob Allen. "And he didn't even acknowledge my existence. I was so embarrassed. I've never felt so small in my life." She did enjoy meeting Carl Perkins, however, who was "great, just as nice as he could be," adding, "I'd love to have a picture of me and him."

In April Reba appeared in *Playboy*—in a manner of speaking. Actually, the magazine just reviewed her album *My Kind of Country*, saying Reba "can transform a Porsche into a pickup—musically speaking—for anyone genetically predisposed to enjoy an honest country voice and relatively traditional instrumentation. She's the mistress of melancholy performing on a small stage in a rural night club on the wet side of the county line, where you can buy 3.2 beer or bring your own bottle."

She was also getting some exposure in the media through commercials. In May she appeared in television ads for the Gold Medal Chevy Dealers Association in Tennessee, promoting pickup trucks and stick shift cars.

Reba had decided for the moment not to do videos, because "we did a lot of research on the subject of country videos, and it became obvious that they are not influencing the record-buying public at all. We've decided not to bother. With the cost involved, they'll have to pay off before we venture into them."

Reba had settled into a comfortable arrangement with Bill Carter, Charlie, and herself managing her career jointly. "We all sit down together and plot out every step, or pick the right individual we need to make moves for us," she said.

She was gathering up ambition as she was gathering up steam and momentum. "The day will come when it will feel right to slack off a bit and settle down," she said. "But it's more exciting now than I ever dreamed it could be. There's always room for more achievement and growth. It's very satisfying for me to be backstage at awards shows and visit with the people who influenced my career. Over the past two years I've been fortunate enough to develop friendships with a lot of them."

But about her newfound fame and success, she was still a bit cautious. "I'm just glad people still want to talk to me," she said. "I still need the people and the publicity and their attention as much as I did before the awards. I just treat people like I want to be treated. I don't want to embarrass anybody and refuse an autograph or refuse to talk to 'em or something like that. All the people in my organization are the same way. We know that it's the people and their loyalty that put us where we are—and we also know that somebody can come along in a New York second and take our place."

CHAPTER 46

The country music industry was still struggling economically; overall sales of country music had dropped 30 percent in late 1983 and 1984. It was noted that pop crossover acts such as Crystal Gayle, Barbara Mandrell, and Mickey Gilley were experiencing sharp sales drops, while performers who persisted in making traditional country music, like Ricky Skaggs, George Strait, and John Anderson, were among the few whose record sales were actually improving.

One reporter went further to note, "It's a measure of just how insincere the crossover wing of the country industry has always been that, now that sales figures are taking a nose dive, *Billboard* reports the major record labels are encouraging their artists to 'go traditional.' "

Reba's foray into traditional country was certainly paying off, and she was gladly tooting her own horn. "I'm basically the only female artist doing traditional country music right now," she said. "I listened to recent hard-country records by guys like Ricky Skaggs and George Strait and thought, 'Why can't a female do this?'"

Her Female Vocalist of the Year award from the CMA, followed by the release of *My Kind of Country*, had seen her emerge as the top female "new traditionalist" in country music, an area that had previously been dominated by male singers. She had begun to catch some flak about her comments on country music; she countered, "I get into a lot of trouble sometimes. I say stuff that I shouldn't say, and people get on me about it, and I say, 'Well, it was the truth!' So, you know, I get in trouble. But I'd rather tell the truth than not."

There is no shortage of big egos in country music, and Reba had pointed that out on "Nashville Now." But she had not received any criticism from that. "That didn't get me in trouble. That was the truth—very much the truth," she said. "There are a lot of artists who've got egos so big that you can't get close to 'em. I mean, you literally can't walk up to 'em and speak, because they won't speak to you."

And things hadn't changed with her success. "The people who did that to me before are pretty much the same," she said. "And I don't really care, 'cause I'm not gonna waste my time on 'em. I feel like everybody in this business, whether they're songwriters, or singers, or what some people refer to as superstars, we're all the same. I've seen that especially since I've been coming to Nashville a lot more. We're all creative people, and God gave us a talent that we're all usin'. It's just that some people get bigger breaks than others. But if you have patience, and you're willing to hang in there, your break will come. 'Good things come to those who wait.' I've always been a firm believer in that. I don't like people who think they're better than you, just because they've had bigger breaks."

But she also defended country music, saying, "People have problems, and they go to hear country music because that's what country music is all about, like family situations that aren't working out. It's life, good or bad. Younger people are going through things today that I didn't hit until I was twenty-one. The sex is what bothers me—the songs, the movies, the TV. When I was a kid, Lucy and Ricky slept in separate beds. Nowadays, women are taking their clothes off on TV. I don't have children, but I don't think I could sit in a room and watch that stuff with my parents, much less my kids. I don't think I'm ready for that. Maybe that's why I don't have kids!"

CHAPTER 47

Harold Shedd had been listed as producer for the *My Kind of Country* album, because he worked with Reba in the studio after she had selected the songs. For the next album, *Have I Got a Deal*, Reba received credit as coproducer, working with Jimmy Bowen in an arrangement that suited them both.

Bowen's role was first to encourage Reba to be herself, act as a sounding board for the songs, then assist in the technical aspects of actually recording the album. "Jimmy does the technical end of it," said Reba. "He sits in there and mixes it—makes sure that everybody blends and the sound is right and the knobs are turned right and all that kind of stuff. I go in with the musicians and decide how it's going to jell together and what musicians are going to lay down what parts."

To gather material for the album, Reba said, "I went out and listened for songs, and then I put all the tapes—including the ones I'd written—together in the order of an album sequence. Then when Jimmy and I was listenin' to 'em together, he said, 'I like this one ["She's the One Loving You Now"] because of the tempo.' I said, 'You really like it?' and he said, 'Yeah.' I said. 'Me and David [Anthony] and Leigh [Reynolds, the guitarists in her band] wrote it.' So he bragged on it a little bit, and then my song, the one I wrote by myself ["Only in My Mind"] came on and he told me he was proud of me. It wasn't like 'Oh, well, if you wrote it, everybody'll think that's the only reason we recorded it.' Because he gave me the okay before I told him it was mine, I had the guts to put it in. I feel pretty good about it."

Loretta Lynn and Emmylou Harris wrote the liner notes for *Have I Got a Deal*. "It was my idea," said Reba. "I wanted the two favorites of mine to be on my album. I asked my producer if it would be okay. He said, 'Why?' Well, one represents the older standards of music: Loretta Lynn's always been the epitome of country music to me; she's the one I've listened to all my life. And Emmylou is a real good friend of mine; I've always loved her singing and what she stands for. It was a huge honor for me."

Discussing *Have I Got a Deal*, Reba said, "In one way, though, there's a lot more of that Dolly influence on this new album, with all her little trills and just the looseness of her vocal cords. When we were making the album, Jimmy said, 'Get out there and sing. Have a good time.' And I just felt so completely at ease with the musicians that he selected. It wasn't like they were studio pickers and I was a vocalist come in to cut an album. After about the first hour, we were like a band and the singer that had been together for three or four months. It gave me a lot of freedom."

Have I Got a Deal for You opens with "I'm in Love All Over," an up-tempo, funky number about true love's joy. "She's Single Again" opens with a single acoustic guitar before Reba delivers the warning to watch out for a man-stealing, good-looking woman on the loose. "The Great Divide" tells the story of a grand canyon between two people, while "Have I Got a Deal for You" is a jaunty song about a lady offering her heart at a bargain. The gentleman in "Red Roses (Won't Work Now)," which closes side 1, has stepped over the line too far too often.

"Only in My Mind," written by Reba, opens side 2. When her husband questions her fidelity, the singer admits her mind has been wandering but, so far, her body has stayed put. The woman in the lively "She's the One Loving You Now," written by Reba with David Anthony and Leigh Reynolds, has lost her man to another woman who wasn't better but was there. "Whose Heartache Is This Anyway?" has twin fiddles and a honky-tonk steel backing up the message that the singer doesn't want advice or philosophy from someone else, she'd rather suffer through it all herself. "I Don't Need Nothin' You Ain't Got" rejects material possessions for true love, while "Don't Forget Your Way Home" lets a lover loose while reminding him of the good deal waiting at home, reminding him that home is where, when you go there, they have to take you back.

When *Have I Got a Deal for You* came out, it was reviewed in *People*, which said, "McEntire shows how well she has mastered the considerable art of sounding devastated and defiant at the same time."

In *Country Music*, reviewer Kip Kirby said, "In a world where plasticity runs rampant and artificiality parades as authenticity, McEntire stands out like sheet silver in a box of Reynolds Wrap. She wrings feeling from lyrics like they're damp Kleenex, bending her almost-yodel vocals around phrases until they're spent. In contrast to the surface flippancy of its title, *Have I Got a Deal for You* contains the kind of substance that once fed the souls of country fans before techno-synthesized slickness turned commerciality into a dirty world."

CHAPTER 48

Reba's personal life was happy, and she was thankful for Charlie. "Our marriage and the business have grown together," she said. "And we've learned all about it together. I think that it's a real good way to do it. Charlie has a real good sense of business and I'm kind of flighty, and it's worked out real well."

She added, "I probably wouldn't have married him if I had sensed that he wouldn't encourage me to go on and do what I wanted to do."

Charlie was traveling with her when he could, although, as Reba said, "In the spring and fall, his cattle demand his time. But when his cattle are out on the grass, he goes out with me."

They had leased an additional fourteen thousand acres. "It's not a bunch of grassland," said Reba. "It's Rocky Mountain country"—a slight exaggeration, though southeastern Oklahoma *is* hilly—"so you need more land to graze cattle. That's Charlie's operation. I'm just a hired hand when I go home. That's where I get my relaxation."

She said she was keeping a level head "just so the tail doesn't get to waggin' the dog." She could feel stardom coming on, she knew she was on the right track and things were clicking into place. It felt good and there was no apprehension on her part, just clear the tracks, full steam ahead. "You can't be frightened when you're just doing what you're meant to do," she said.

She pooh-poohed the idea of fame going to her head. "It's somethin' that won't be a problem," she said. "If I ever have the least indication of egotism or the big head, they [family and friends] will slap me down to size real quick. We're a family and we remember where we came from. When I go back, I'm a neighbor. I'm not a star or celebrity. If anything, I'm just a twinkle."

A few years before she had said, "I want to get in the big leagues and have a good sound and give people their money's worth. I want to satisfy 'em." Well, she was doing it now.

As for her goals, she said, "The biggest goal in my life is to not make a big mistake. The little ones you can get away with and learn from. But my biggest goal is to not make that big mistake, 'cause it'll kill you. It'll set you back. And in this business you can't afford that."

CHAPTER 49

Reba continued working hard on her live shows, trying to make them better. She admitted at the beginning of the year, "We're very dedicated to this career. If I want to relax I go shoppin'—but I'm shoppin' for show clothes."

She said about performing, "I crave it. It's just like you'd crave food or enjoy going to bed or watching a good movie. It's just something that I was meant to do. What it does for me I don't know; it's just like having a good friend out there. It's a part of my life that I really enjoy."

She had raised the prices of her live performances a bit in 1985, but was quick to defend this. "We've heard some good feedback at the shows," she said. "But we didn't raise our prices because of it. Before the awards show at the first of the year, we had already set our goal to raise our price a little bit. After we won the award, that's all it was raised. We didn't jack our prices up five or six thousand dollars just because I won that award. I have heard of some people winning an award and then jumping their concert price ten thousand dollars overnight. Some can get away with it. But it all comes down to, you're only worth how many tickets you can sell or how many records you can sell. I don't want to shoot myself out of a bunch of jobs by overpricing myself. I'd like to be in the business longer than that."

On the question of why she toured so much, she answered, "The best way I can answer that question is, when people see me perform sometimes they say, 'Golly, you're nothing like your records,' or 'I want to go buy your records now.' There's some kind of personality that I haven't been portraying on my records that I do portray in a concert situation.

"That's what my producer, Jimmy Bowen, and I have been working on," she continued. "We record in one week and we do it with the same band. We try to get a feel of a live show. We try to get that excitement and energy that we get at a live show and put it on record. It helps so much because you get that one-on-one attention to a fan out there—or a nonfan that you're trying to convert to be a fan. That makes a big difference. They either like you, love you, or hate you by the time they leave. They've got to change their feelings about you one way or another."

She did miss some things out on the road and admitted that during the summer "we were so hungry for pinto beans, fried taters, soft tomatoes, and corn bread, and we couldn't find that where they were."

In answer to the question of how she kept so trim, she answered, "I wear tight Wranglers."

CHAPTER 50

In October 1985 Reba was nominated for Entertainer of the Year as well as Female Vocalist of the Year by the Country Music Association.

When Bill Carter had first called and told her of the Entertainer of the Year listing (she was nominated with Alabama, Lee Greenwood, Ricky Skaggs, and George Strait), she teased a little bit. "I kinda asked him, 'Do you mean that big award they give out at the last of the show?' she remembered. When he said yes, "I started screaming and hollerin' all over the place." She told the next reporter she saw, "I am shocked and totally tickled."

Indeed, 1985 was the year "country" came back to country music, as reflected in the CMA Awards. There was a special segment honoring Patsy Cline and performances by Ricky Skaggs, Loretta Lynn, Emmylou Harris, Ray Price, Johnny Cash, and Merle Haggard. George Strait won the Male Vocalist of the Year award, and the Judds were the Group of the Year.

Ricky Skaggs, who had begun the "new traditionalist" movement back in 1980 after leaving Emmylou Harris's band, took home the Entertainer trophy, but Reba won her second CMA award for Female Vocalist.

Accepting her award, Reba said, "Jimmy Bowen let me do my kind of music. That gave me more of a chance to look inside myself and figure out what I wanted to do. And I can't tell you how good I feel about that. I think it was very, very important."

She grew tearful when she accepted the award and said, "God likes me when I work, but he loves me when I sing. We thank you from the bottom of our hearts for letting us continue to do what the Lord let us do."

After the show, Reba said, "It's a good night for country music. The songs that George Strait, Ricky Skaggs, and Reba McEntire are singing are the backbone of country music. It's what the public and the industry wants to hear and see today."

Reba admitted, "Last year, I just kicked back and had a good time, because I didn't think I had a chance to win. But tonight I was much more nervous, 'cause, honestly, I thought I did have a chance."

After the CMA Awards, Reba sang the national anthem at the opening game of the World Series in Kansas City on Saturday, October 19. But she couldn't stay to watch the game; after the singing, she flew eighty miles by helicopter to Ottawa, Kansas, where she had a concert.

CHAPTER 51

Reba's career was off and running, but she was still not selling as many albums as she wanted—was not even selling as many albums as most expect a CMA winner to sell. This bothered her, and she thought long and hard on it. One day she and Bill Carter were talking, analyzing her career, and she asked, "Why do the men generally outsell the women?" Their conclusion: "It's because the men are selling to women." The next question: Who was buying Reba McEntire albums?

That question was more difficult—Reba honestly didn't know. She went to her label and they began doing research to determine her audience. She also made a conscious decision: find songs women could relate to and cultivate an audience of women fans.

She had begun to think about the country music audience and said, "Most country fans are women—who don't like feeling threatened. The true country queens are those who bond most intimately with their female fans."

She added that "I don't want their husbands. I can just barely handle my own. I want to be those women's friend. You know, they've got problems. Like if I was a woman whose husband was cheatin' on me, or who worked nine to five, sick to death of my job, sick to death of the kids, sick to death of my husband, sick to death of what I'm havin' to go through—that's the kind of songs I pick. There's a lot of women out there who just want to have that three minutes of rebellion."

One of the first things she did to appeal to women was change her way of dressing. "I quit wearing spandex pants," she said, "Because, although they're the most comfortable britches I've ever had on, since they stretch, I thought women might be offended by me walking out there in a pair of tight pants. So I went to western skirts and boots." But that didn't work because "I wasn't comfortable with that, I couldn't get down, get sassy with them the way I wanted to. So I went back to the britches, which I feel is more me. I hardly ever wear dresses, and I don't feel honest onstage wearing a dress."

Being honest was important to her, and she felt the way she dressed was part of that. "Another part of being honest is not being phony in any way," she said. "If my throat goes dry and I mess up and have to quit, I just wave at them and say, 'I'll be back with you in a minute.' I've tripped over microphone cords, I've stumbled, I've fallen down and forgotten words, but they love it if you're honest and open with them. But if you try to hide it, they'll crucify you."

Along the way she found that you could appeal to both men and women "if you find the best songs possible" and that she did not have to lose old fans—or, in this case, male fans—in order to attract new ones. "If you don't come out there in a negligee with everything you got showing, you're not going to tick the women off," she said. "Now I don't want to tick anybody off. I want to be everybody's friend. I mean, I've always wanted to be accepted."

She had begun to assert herself in subtle, though definite, ways. In the spring she cut her shoulder-length hair into a shorter, more modern, more comfortable look. "Two years ago, I don't know if I would've had the nerve to do it by myself, not without asking if it was okay," she said.

She had made an appointment in McAlester with Tandy, her hairdresser. She was preparing for her normal trim, but Tandy said he thought Reba would benefit from a shortened style of hair, like Barbara Mandrell had done. "I told him to go ahead. So he did," said Reba.

Charlie wasn't pleased. "When I walked out, Charlie wouldn't talk to me," she said. "He'd just look at me and shake his head, like 'I can't believe you did that.' He just hated it." Later, she said, he liked it fine.

Increasingly, Reba wanted to appeal to female fans. She had realized that the most successful female singers sang for their fans, serving as a spokeswoman for them. The best female country singers had bonded with their female fans, saying things they wanted to say to their husbands or boyfriends or men in general, but couldn't. Success was what drove Reba more than anything else, the desire to be successful, the top female singer in country music. And so she increasingly looked for songs that spoke to women, and she made a conscious decision to record an album that every female could relate to.

She had viewed herself as a country singer up until now. Now she began viewing herself as a female country singer. She knew there was a place for female country singers, a unique place in country music. And there would always be one or two female singers who would emerge as the best of their time. Reba wanted to be that female singer. But she needed the songs. So she set about looking for them all throughout 1985 for the album she would record in the fall. It was a gamble, but she wanted to take it; the only way to get the big record sales, the big crowds at concerts, to have her face and name known throughout the nation was to take this chance. The big questions were Would it work, and could she—Reba McEntire—be the top female country singer of her time?

CHAPTER 52

When Cecil Sharp, an Englishman, made his historic trip into the mountain communities of Tennessee and North Carolina in 1914–16, he discovered a number of old British folk songs still sung, in much the same manner they had always been sung, by the descendents of English and Scottish settlers who had come there as long as two centuries earlier. Sharp transcribed songs such as "The Sheffield Apprentice," "Little Musgrave and Lady Barnard," and "The Gypsy Laddie" on his trips. Those songs had originally been collected and categorized by Francis Child in England and Scotland (and are usually referred to as "Child ballads").

Later, collectors came to the same regions and recorded those songs on early recording devices. They discovered that men were more likely to play instruments—the fiddle was most popular—and form bands, but the women were most likely to sing. Those women usually sang those songs unaccompanied in their home, carrying on the oral tradition that had begun centuries before. Thus the woman was usually the key link in preserving the songs and passing them along to her children, who would pass them down to still another generation.

As the country music industry developed and grew in the 1920s, women singers and musicians were rare. This was a traditional culture, and the traditional role for the woman was in the home, raising the family. They still sang, and many learned instruments, but their songs were usually heard only in the home.

To a certain extent, the Carter Family changed that. The Carter women—Maybelle and Sara—were instrumental in carrying the traditional folk songs into the mainstream of country music in the late 1920s and up to World War II.

First recorded in Bristol, Virginia, in August 1927 by Ralph Peer, the Carters sang songs they had grown up hearing. Because Ralph Peer was a publisher as well as a record company executive working with Victor, he copyrighted the songs and listed the singer—or, in this case, A. P. Carter—as the writer. Thus the Carters are credited with writing songs such as "Wildwood Flower," "Hello, Stranger," "You Are My Flower," "Jimmie Brown the Newsboy," "I'm Thinking Tonight of My Blue Eyes," and "Worried Man Blues." Although A. P. Carter did write some songs, he was primarily an astute folk song collector who received credit as writer of these songs because of the business acumen of Ralph Peer.

The Carter Family never really performed much—mostly in small schoolhouses and churches in the Maces Springs area of Virginia where they lived, as well as in the neighboring states of North Carolina and Kentucky—and they certainly could not be considered a touring act. In fact, the Carters always had to find work outside music for their primary income, and in 1929 A. P. moved to Detroit to work in factories while Maybelle and her husband, Ezra, moved to Washington, D.C. They would get together only to rehearse and record.

The Carters' recordings sold well during the Great Depression—the only country act besides Jimmie Rodgers to do so—even though Sara and A. P. divorced in 1932. In the period from 1936 to 1938 all three moved to San Antonio, Texas, where they performed on radio there as well as on border stations around Del Rio. Their twice-daily radio shows there led to the Carters' music being heard for the first time outside the South.

The Carter Family finally disbanded in 1943. By that time, Maybelle had become one of the most influential guitar players in country music, with her style of hitting the bass notes with her thumb while brushing the rest of the strings with her fingers. This allowed her to pick out the melody on the bass strings while the other strings provided a full chordal and rhythmic accompaniment.

Sara always sang lead, although by the end of their career, she and Maybelle had established a memorable duet style. A. P. was the driving force in the group, finding the songs, overseeing rehearsals, and getting them to recording dates. But his divorce from Sara apparently took the wind out of his sails. In addition, A. P. needed Sara's vocals and Maybelle's guitar playing to be a successful act.

Sara was never particularly ambitious—she could either take music or leave it. And when the Carters disbanded, she simply went to California with her new husband (a cousin of A. P.'s she married in 1939) and lived a quiet life. Maybelle, however, had developed a great deal of ambition along the way, and when the original Carter Family disbanded, Maybelle formed a group with her daughters and became part of the country music community in Nashville.

The Carter women could become successful in country music because they were part of a family. Sara and A. P. were married—at least at first—and Maybelle was their sister-in-law. They were always known as the Carter *Family*—their act embraced traditional family values, including the traditional view of a woman's role. Although the women were more prominent on recordings, it was A. P. who clearly ran the show and whose name was on all the songs.

The first million seller by a female country singer was "I Want to Be a Cowboy's Sweetheart" by Patsy Montana in 1936. But the first female country music star was Kitty Wells. Born Muriel Deason, she was married to Johnny Wright, a member of the popular duo Johnny and Jack. Wright gave her the moniker Kitty Wells after the folk song "The Ballad of Kitty Wells."

Wells was also the beneficiary of the "family" tradition, singing on shows with her husband and traveling together to appearances. That tradition allowed her to remain a "respectable" woman while traveling with mostly male entourages in cramped cars from town to town.

There were other women in country music—Rose Maddox of the Maddox Brothers and Sister Rose act as well as Minnie Pearl, for example—but Kitty's hit "It Wasn't God Who Made Honky Tonk Angels" in 1952 ushered in the era of the woman singer in country music.

"It Wasn't God Who Made Honky Tonk Angels" was an answer song, a popular device in country music in which the singer responds to a previous song. The original song was "Wild Side of Life," a hit for Hank Thompson earlier in 1952 (both recordings would sell a million copies that year) where the singer laments that the woman he married wasn't meant to be a good wife because she had been lured away by the honky-tonks. The message was clear—some women just had bad blood, and even a good marriage to a good man couldn't change that.

Kitty's answer presented another side, saying that too many married men strayed and behaved like they were single, causing many a good girl to go wrong. Instead of the original's lament, "I never knew God made honky-tonk angels," Kitty countered that it wasn't God but hell-bent men who made them. At last, a spokesperson for the woman's point of view.

(Ironically, a new version of "Wild Side of Life" by Maurey Finney was at number 84 in May 1976, when Reba made her debut on the charts. There was no new version of the answer song, though.)

CHAPTER 53

When Reba McEntire was born—on March 28, 1955—there were six songs with a woman singing on the *Billboard* folk charts, and Kitty Wells was on three of those. Furthermore, she was the only female soloist—the other three records were duets. (At that time, *Billboard* listed only fifteen songs on each chart—sales, jukebox play, and radio airplay—and labeled country music "folk music.")

That was a major change from the year before, when Kitty Wells was the only woman on the country music charts. In fact, only one woman is listed among the Top Twenty country artists of the 1950s: Kitty Wells. And that was an improvement over the 1940s, when not a single woman made the Top Twenty.

A few women were on the pop charts, however. The McGuire Sisters had the top-selling recording, "Sincerely." The pop charts had discovered female singers (generally called "thrushes," "warblers," and "gals" by *Billboard*) before country music did.

Million sellers in 1954 included Rosemary Clooney's "This Ole House," the Chordettes' "Mister Sandman," and albums by Doris Day and Judy Garland. That era is marked by the white middle-class market's desire to hear both country music and black music—as long as it was sung by white pop singers. Thus Rosemary Clooney, Patti Page, Georgia Gibbs, and others were having hits with songs borrowed from Nashville (particularly by Hank Williams) and from the black market.

Throughout the 1960s the traditional role of the woman was both reinforced and challenged by women country music singers. Loretta Lynn, the major female star to emerge during that decade, beginning with her first chart record in 1961, sang "Don't Come Home A'Drinkin' (With Lovin' on Your Mind)," "You Ain't Woman Enough to Take My Man," and the autobiographical "Your Squaw's on the Warpath." Tammy Wynette sang "Stand by Your Man," but her private life was more reflective of the message "Don't Stand by Your Men." Especially when they weren't a-doin' you right.

That, of course, reflected the social changes of the 1960s, as the Eisenhower 1950s—where the ideal women were Donna Reed, Harriet Nelson, or June Allyson—gave way to a more feisty, independent woman. Here the woman was not locked in a marriage her whole life. Whether it was her choice or the husband's doings, D-I-V-O-R-C-E was part of life, and country music reflected that.

In May 1976, when Reba made her debut on the *Billboard* country chart with her first single, "I Don't Want to Be a One Night Stand," hers was one of twenty-five records with a female singer (including duets and groups) then on the chart. Included in the Top Ten were Emmylou Harris, Crystal Gayle, Olivia Newton-John, Billie Jo Spears, and Mary Lou Turner (in a duet with Bill Anderson).

Each of the major female country singers in the past had portrayed a certain type of woman. Kitty Wells, as the first, broke a lot of ground voicing the woman's point of view, but she

161

primarily represented the traditional female. Patsy Cline represented the woman as a great artist, more independent than Kitty Wells, with a talent that could rival—and surpass—any man's. Still, her biggest hits were songs in which a vulnerable woman was the victim of a man's whims.

Although her main influence was Patsy Cline, Loretta Lynn's down-home folksiness made her a successor to Kitty Wells, a traditional woman singing from a woman's point of view. But from her very first record, "Honky Tonk Girl," Lynn carved out a persona more independent and feisty than Wells or Cline could have hoped for. Many of her numbers were answer songs not to individual hits but to whole genres—"Don't Come Home A'Drinkin' " to the barroom ballad, "You Ain't Woman Enough" to the cheatin' song. Tammy Wynette personified female vulnerability almost to the point of masochism, though on occasion she could threaten, "Your Good Girl's Gonna Go Bad."

Dolly Parton was the first country female superstar, the first who could compete outside Nashville. Many of Patsy Cline's hits had climbed high on the pop charts, but neither she nor any other female country singer enjoyed Dolly's huge success in the larger market. Indeed, Dolly Parton has perhaps reached further than any other country female, but as a result has transcended the country category. That has been both a blessing and a curse; she has taken country music and her own career to new heights, but in doing so can no longer be considered strictly a country singer. Dolly has become a popular culture icon.

Emmylou Harris, a latter-day Patsy Cline, once again represents the woman as a great artist, with a talent to match any male singer's. Unlike Cline, Harris, a beneficiary of the outlaw movement, has been able to exercise an artistic control over her albums unprecedented among female country artists. Ironically, among Emmylou's influences are the most traditional country styles; musically, she is closer to Kitty Wells than to Patsy Cline.

More than any other artist—male or female—it was Emmylou Harris who really began the "new traditionalist" movement in country music. When she had her first hit on the country charts in 1974 with the old Louvin Brothers song "If I Could Only Win Your Love," it signaled a new respect for the old music. It was Emmylou who made the past respectable and brought country music history before a wider audience. It was she who gave Ricky Skaggs a platform and encouragement to launch his own career in 1980, which marked the beginning of new traditionalism as a major force in country music of the 1980s.

After Ricky Skaggs, who came from the bluegrass tradition and the mountains of Kentucky, came George Strait, from the honky-tonk and western swing tradition of Texas. These two established the new traditionalist movement. After Skaggs and Strait, there was a place for a female singer in the movement, and that is where Reba McEntire stepped in, especially with her *My Kind of Country* album in 1985.

CHAPTER 54

On Tuesday, January 14, 1986, Reba was seen joining the Grand Ole Opry during a television special—the first artist ever to join on a TV broadcast instead of during a regular performance. She sang "Somebody Should Leave" during the telecast. That Friday night, January 17, the sixty-first member of the Opry made her "official" debut premiering her song "Whoever's in New England."

Joining the Opry was a thrill for her. "People there were wantin' their picture made with me," she said. "And there was Dolly and Loretta and Willie and all the big stars of the Grand Ole Opry! And I was sayin'—I got kinda irritated—'Don't bother about me: there's Loretta and Dolly!' 'Cause I was a fan of theirs. It was like, 'Don't be silly; there's Kitty Wells and Roy Acuff. Go take their picture.' It was then I realized, 'Hey Reba, now I am somebody.' But I still ran around all night and took pictures myself. I had a ball!"

Whoever's in New England was released in January and features a very pretty, mature Reba on the cover, dressed in a brown country dress, wearing her rodeo belt buckle, in front of a weatherbeaten barn.

The album begins with "Can't Stop Now," an up-tempo song about falling head first into love. In the next number, "You Can Take the Wings off Me," a basically conservative girl wants to pick up the tempo in her life. The faithful wife in "Whoever's in New England" suspects her executive husband's frequent trips to Boston aren't all business; still she'll welcome him back when he's through with his fling, or when his fling is through with him.

Others may be telling her she'll get over her lover, but the singer in "I'll Believe It When I Feel It" isn't buying that line. Side 1 closes with "I've Seen Better Days," a down-and-out ballad about being out in the cold.

"Little Rock," which opens side 2, is a bouncy song about slippin' off the diamond ring and flying from the high life in search of true love. "If You Only Knew" is a song by two women—Diana Rae and Jane Mariash—that states simply and clearly that the single life ain't all it's cracked up to be. In a western shuffle, "One Thin Dime," Reba says to just call her and she'll be waiting: even a good man may stray sometimes, but a good woman always waits faithfully.

"Don't Touch Me There" addresses someone who touches her body but leaves her heart alone. "Don't Make That Same Mistake Again" is a honky-tonk number where the singer says she'd gladly fall for this feller and make a fool of herself all over again.

When it came out, Reba told a reporter the album "is a more serious, emotional album to me. I don't know if it was the time of the year, or the mood I was in, or what. But I cut some pretty deep emotional kinds of songs—they kinda rip you up a little bit."

164

She and coproducer Jimmy Bowen had developed a good system for her recording sessions. "What I usually do is find most of the songs I'm going to record," said Reba. "And then I let my band learn them, and I do 'em in my live show and live with 'em a couple of months. Then, in the studio, when the session musicians get familiar with the song and go in the studio to lay down the instrumental tracks, I'll go in and sing with 'em. That way, they feed off me and I feed off them, and we get more feeling that way. I don't like to just go in and add the vocal to a prerecorded music track. As a safety precaution, I usually stay in there after the musicians have finished, and sing it over again three or four more times, in case I made a boo-boo or something on the live track. But we usually end up going with the live track, because there's just that extra feeling there."

On January 30 Reba was in Boston, filming her first video for the single "Whoever's in New England." Directing the video was Jon Small for his Manhattan-based company, Picture Vision.

On Thursday, Small and his crew of eighteen shot the finale first, at Boston's Logan Airport. Here Reba met her "husband," Boston actor/model Robert Riley, for the first time. This sequence of the video features McEntire singing in the airport crowd. On the first take, she sang with such full-throated intensity, tears welling in her eyes, that the crew and ticket agents applauded spontaneously.

Small wanted Reba to begin with singing, since that was what she was most comfortable with. When that sequence was finished, the cast and crew went to the Park Plaza Hotel, where Riley and Boston model Beverly Prater acted out McEntire's "fantasy" of a romantic candlelight dinner.

At sunset everyone was outside, shivering in the fifteen-degree weather as Riley and Prater tossed snow at each other. Since there wasn't enough real snow on Boston Common, there were two boxes of fake snow added to the ground.

The next morning at 6 A.M. everyone was en route to New Bedford, about an hour south of Boston, for a shot of Reba's "home." Professional artists John Thornton and Pat Coomey would receive $290 for the use of their historic 1840 carriage house for a half day. But first they had to be placated, and manager Bill Carter charmed them well, getting Reba to pose for photos with the couple to help ease their fears about a camera crew invading their home.

Take after take wore everyone down, and at the 3:30 lunch break tempers flared. A drive to the airport by Reba and her "husband" came next as the crew stood outside in the freezing weather. Then the locale shifted to a bank in New Bedford for the corporate boardroom set, where evening light was used as morning light.

On Saturday morning Reba flew out to a performance in Illinois while Small and his crew went to Windsor Total Video in New York and transferred the film to videotape. The crew worked at the $500-an-hour facility six hours on Monday and again on Tuesday before sending copies of the finished video to Bill Carter in Nashville and the MCA headquarters in Los Angeles.

On Wednesday Reba and Carter watched the video. Six nights later it premiered on "Entertainment Tonight" to a national audience. This was Reba's first video, and she started with a killer; when all was said and done, this video would do more for her career than any other single appearance or performance to date.

Back in New York, Jon Small was effusive in his praise for Reba. Small had worked with a number of major acts, but noted that Reba was the first to autograph albums for the cast and crew to take home and to provide a handwritten thank-you note for everyone after the filming was done. "I like that lady," said Small. "As soon as she walked up to me and slapped me on the back and said, 'Hi, I'm Reba,' I thought to myself, 'This is one good gal.' "

CHAPTER 55

On February 22, 1986, the single, "Whoever's in New England," entered the *Billboard* charts; it would be Reba's third number one record. But more important, it would be her "career" song, the one on which she would become an established star. It was followed by the snappy, up-tempo "Little Rock," which also peaked at number one, and then "What Am I Gonna Do About You."

This last single would also reach number one. It was released in October, in prime time for Christmas sales. Labels traditionally save their big guns for May and October releases: May for the summer buyers and October for the Christmas crowd. With this album, Reba McEntire became one of the music industry's big guns.

"Whoever's in New England" was probably the first country song with "Massachusetts" in the first line. And going to Boston for a business trip is not typical fare for a country song topic. But talking about "Whoever's in New England," Reba said, "I know girls in Oklahoma and Texas and Florida whose husbands go to Boston all the time for business meetings. It's an easy song to relate to.

"The song is all about a woman's imagination. I've gone through the same thing when my husband was in the rodeo. I'd be sitting around thinking, 'What's he doing tonight? Where is he?' Then I'd call his hotel, but he wouldn't be there. So you get a roaming imagination even though he might just be on his way back to the hotel."

In April Reba and Charlie managed to get back to their ranch in Stringtown for a few days. Charlie and his crew were outside roping and branding cattle while Reba was inside the kitchen cooking up dinner. "I love to do that kind of thing," said Reba. "I'm not on a star trip; when I'm at home I like to eat, so I'll just get the skillet down and fry up some ham and sliced potatoes or something for our breakfast"—or, in this case, a whole dinner for the crew.

But, she added, "I can only take about a week of that at a time, then I start to get ready to go back out there doin' my music." Actually, Reba would not have even a week at home this time. She would spend the afternoon visiting the throat doctor, making some deposits at the bank, and stopping at the cleaners to get a fresh batch of clothes for the road.

Reba was working hard on her career, saying, "I don't feel like I'm on top yet, just because I've won a couple of awards. We've still got a lot of work ahead of us, and me and Charlie realize it.

"There's still plenty of places where I'm unknown—on record sales, on ticket sales, on face visibility, on everything. We've just got our foot in the door. The way I look at it now, it's 'Let's kick this into high gear!' "

How far she had to go was demonstrated to her early in the year as she sat in a Mexican restaurant on West Forty-eighth Street in New York, sipping a margarita on the rocks while nobody around was staring. "Dadgummit, I'm going to change that," she said. "I want people up here to know me by my face." Talking about awards and success she was adamant: "I'm greedy now. I want it all."

She had a taste of the big time in the spring at the Academy of Country Music show, when she won her second Female Vocalist of the Year award. She also cohosted the nationally televised event, along with John Schneider and Mac Davis. Reba was obviously pleased, enthusing, "Golly! We must be doin' something right!"

CHAPTER 56

"**Y**ou've got to be a gypsy at heart to live this kind of life," said Reba about life on the road. And she was right, as she performed a series of one-nighters all through 1986.

"It's hard, following a timetable and staying in a positive mood," she noted. "And it's hard being away from my family." But Charlie was with her a good deal of the time, and Reba noted, "Charlie's my best friend. And I'm glad he's with me."

Talking about Charlie, she said, "He don't like any of the limelight. Charlie don't want any attention. The only reason he got into my career was because I needed him to so desperately.

"He's a good money manager," she added. "He knows when we need something. I just spend money. I love to spend money. See, I want more constantly in the way of a lighting director, backdrops, staging, all this kinda stuff. And he says, 'No. We can't go beyond our means. We've got to take it one step at a time and grow gradually.' And that just drives me nuts. I want it now!"

She admitted, "Charlie thinks I'm too competitive. But I have to have somebody I'm in competition with all the time. You just have to have goals, and competition helps that."

Discussing her family, she said that after she won her last Female Vocalist of the Year award, her mother called and said, "We're as proud of you as parents can be, something you'll never know until you have kids of your own." "Mothers just never give up," said Reba, smiling. But she wasn't planning on motherhood. "I was a rodeo brat and went all over the country in the back seat of a car," she said. "I don't want my kids to do that, and I don't want somebody else to raise my kids. I'm just not ready right now to be a mother."

She had said previously, "I'm the only one out of my family

that doesn't have a child. And right now, I don't plan to. It's never been a real strong desire for me."

Still, reporters and fans—as well as her family—kept wondering about her having children; after all, the biological clock was ticking, and she'd turned thirty at the end of March. She said to one reporter, "I'd better be thinking about it, hadn't I? I want children, but I don't know if I want them enough. My schedule is pretty rough as it is." She paused, then added, "But I'm thinking, and I'm sure Charlie's been thinking quite awhile."

She had switched booking agencies, from Headline International to the Jim Halsey Company. At one stop she admitted, "I'm real tired right now, and I'm looking forward to a rest. We've been traveling as many as six or seven hundred miles a night trying to make our schedule."

The demands of stardom were becoming an everyday part of her life. "I enjoy my fans," she said. "But most of them treat me like I'm not a person. I don't feel I deserve that kind of worship. I don't want people to worship me—I just want to entertain them and for them to like what I do.

"It gets a little deep sometimes. I got a thank-you card recently from a man who said one of my songs brought his family together again when they'd been considering a divorce. It's scary when you think how much power you have over people."

She enjoyed signing autographs "when I'm in the mood for it. [But] sometimes I'm just too tired to enjoy it," she confessed.

"You have a lot of sacrifices in this business," she said. "I know a million people who'd love to go to work for me. It looks real glamorous on the outside, but it's just hard work on the inside."

But she was clearly ready to make the sacrifices necessary for stardom. Writer Bob Allen, in a story in *Country Music*, noted, "She's poised to make the leap from queen of the new traditionalists and the industry's most-favored daughter to broad-based superstar." He went on to state, "This will mean even less time spent at home with Charlie. . . . It will mean less time fence riding and cattle roping and resting her vocal chords on the additional thirteen thousand leased acres near Chockie Mountain, where they graze their twelve hundred or so head of Brahman and Hereford cattle. It also means any plans for a family of her own will be postponed, or perhaps put off altogether."

CHAPTER 57

Out on the road a couple of songs had been getting noticed by crowds, especially "Somebody Should Leave" from the *My Kind of Country* album. During the song, Reba often had tears in her eyes, leading some fans to ask about her private life. "People ask me why I've been crying," she told a reporter. "They ask me if I've lost my husband, or if I'm going through a divorce. I just tell 'em the truth—everything's fine."

She remembered the first time she had heard the song, when she and Charlie had gone to Harlan Howard's home in Nashville to listen to some songs. "I'd never met him before," she said, "but Bill Carter called him up and said, 'Can they come over?' and he said, 'Well, sure.'.

"We went over there and was settin' there, and he was playin' me some songs. He said, 'I want to play you this new song, just to see what you think about it.' And I was just settin' back in one of his big ol' high-backed leather chairs, bein' real comfortable. I was kinda thinkin' about dinner, cause it was gettin' close to dinnertime and I was gettin' hungry. This song came on, and I just set up. I hadn't heard this kind of song in years. And when the chorus came, I got all choked up. Then when the ending came, I was cryin'. I said, 'Harlan, can I have that song?' And he said, 'I kinda thought you'd say that.' Because he had written songs for Patsy Cline, and I just loved her, you know. He wants to be buddies. And, man, we were buddies till death do us part by the time we left that house, the way I felt about it. Just to meet him and see what somebody can do. That song will always be a highlight of my life."

It was not hard to cry on that song, she said. "What's hard is to hold it back. But you can really get into it. And people come up to me and say, 'How do you cry every time?' They never ask me if it's fake. But a lot of them come up and say, 'I cried as much as you did.' So that really makes me feel that the song is an honest song."

Discussing that song with reporter Bob Allen, Reba said, "I've never been divorced, but I've been around divorces. Charlie has been, and he's got two children. It's sad. It's horrible. Divorces hurt so many people—for a lifetime, not just for a month or a year. My nieces and nephews have been through a divorce, and sometimes I'll get to singing that song onstage, and I'll think about them babies, remembering when they were kids, hearing the arguments, and it makes me so sad. Sometimes when I sing it, I even forget the audience is there."

In June *Reba Nell McEntire*, a collection of tracks recorded by Polygram, had been released—almost three years after she had left the label. It was intended to capitalize on her MCA success.

The album begins with "I've Never Stopped Dreaming of You," a country ballad about a love who's long gone but the memory lingers on. "Hold On," a song about hanging on to see where love can carry us, follows and next is "I Know I'll Have a Better Day Tomorrow," a gospel song written by Reba. The song states simply that keepin' the faith will keep her keepin' on. "Don't Say Good Night, Say Good Morning" is a bedroom ballad about pulling love through the hard times, and the side closes with an interesting number, "Muddy Mississippi," about a country girl who went to town and now can't live down what she had been livin' up; and so there is a suicide. It is reminiscent of "Fancy" by Bobbi Gentry.

Side 2 opens with "It's Another Silent Night," about lovers not communicating, and is followed by the Ivory Joe Hunter classic

"Empty Arms," a ballad of yearning for love. Again, Reba has her Patsy Cline voice for this one. "Love Is Never Easy" is a popish ballad stating the obvious. "Waitin' for the Sun to Shine," a song of hope and renewal, was a hit for Ricky Skaggs, and "Good Friends" is a ballad about how wonderful it is to have a close friend. This ode to the joy of true friendship closes this album, which did well coming on the heels of the MCA success.

The cover features an early picture of a young Reba, culled from the Polygram files.

In August 1986 Reba filmed her second video, again with Jon Small and Picture Vision. The video featured David Keith, the Tennessee-born actor who appeared in *An Officer and a Gentlemen*, and was shot in Manhattan. The song was "What Am I Gonna Do About You," the title cut from her new album, which was scheduled to be released September 19.

MCA and Bill Carter had arranged for a cross-promotion involving MCA, Jeep, and Camelot Records, a chain that would create floor displays of the album in its stores. Cassettes would be packaged in a "free-with-purchase" case that held ten cassettes and looked like an orange crate. Each case had "Jeep" printed on one end and "Camelot" on the other. The displays would also carry entry blanks for a sweepstakes with a Jeep truck as the grand prize. There were plans to introduce this special promotion, which marked Reba hitting the promotional big time, into the Musicland chain at the end of the year.

Reba visited warehouses and staff meetings of Camelot, Target, Musicland, and Wal-Mart executives and employees. She even did a full-fledged show for Wal-Mart executives.

In addition, she would be featured in *McCall's* in the fall, and

MCA would run a four-color ad in the issue, spotlighting her entire label catalogue.

At that time, Reba was assured of selling about three thousand tickets for a show. *Whoever's in New England* had sold over 325,000 copies thus far, eclipsing *Have I Got a Deal for You*, which had sold about 165,000 copies.

What Am I Gonna Do About You begins with "Why Not Tonight," an up-tempo song with the message to seize the moment. "What Am I Gonna Do About You" is about the inability to get over a past love; Reba embellishes the melody with rapid, Dolly Parton—ish curlicues, sounding emotionally vulnerable all the while. "Lookin' for a New Love Story" is an optimistic song: I think, therefore it'll be; or, if we can dream it, we can do it. "Take Me Back," with its doo-wop, 1950s opening, yearns to recapture sweet golden moments. In "My Mind Is on You," which closes side 1, the singer's mind is on someone while her body is somewhere else; running away was easy, but coming back is difficult.

Side 2 begins with a real roof raiser, "Let the Music Lift You." The message here is that music can cure more than medicine. "I Heard Her Cryin'" is about a child hurt over her parents' fighting. The singer in the fiddle-laced "No Such Thing" denies there's anyone else while pledging undying love to her true love. "One Promise Too Late" is a snappy song of a missed opportunity; the right one came along after vows were made to someone else. The album closes with "Till It Snows in Mexico," a song about basic, traditional values. When a woman takes a husband, it's for life. The singer sees marriage as sacred and forever; she pledges to love her man until it snows in Mexico.

On September 17 Reba had appeared on a special "Nashville Now" segment with her brother, Pake, and sister Susie. Host Ralph Emery, an only child, introduced the show by saying he had always been intrigued about how siblings got along, because he never had any. Reba admitted this show was "for Mama," who was in McAlester at Pake's in-laws watching.

Reba sang "No Such Thing" to open the show. Ralph then pointed out to the audience that Reba had been nominated for five Country Music Association Awards: Single, Video, and Album of the Year (all for "Whoever's in New England"), Female Vocalist, and the big one, Entertainer of the Year. Then Ralph looked at Reba and made a prediction. "I think this is your year," he said. "I think you will be Entertainer of the Year."

The show featured the Singing McEntires doing a gospel song, "Will There Be Any Stars in My Crown," Susie singing a gospel medley—"The Man in the Middle," "Farther Along," and Green Pastures"—Pake doing "Bad Love" and "Heart vs. Heart" (with Reba singing harmony on the last one), and Reba singing "Whoever's in New England" and "Little Rock."

The show contained a big surprise during the call-in section —where fans call and ask questions of the celebrities—when Jackie McEntire appeared on the line. Ralph asked her to describe her children, and Mama McEntire's response was appropriate to those who know her. She described her children as "perfection."

On Monday night, October 13, the Country Music Association held its awards show. Willie Nelson and Kris Kristofferson hosted, and featured performers were Lionel Richie, Earl Thomas Conley, Anita Pointer, Eddie Rabbitt, Marie Osmond, Paul Davis, Juice Newton, Nicolette Larson, and Steve Wariner.

Big winners that night included Randy Travis, who won the Horizon Award, as his star was beginning to rise, and George Strait, who was Male Vocalist of the Year. The Judds were Group of the Year, "On the Other Hand" was Song of the Year, and "Bop" was Single of the Year. Reba came to the stage during the evening to carry home her third consecutive Female Vocalist of the Year trophy.

At the end of the evening, host Kris Kristofferson announced the nominees for Entertainer of the Year: Reba McEntire, Willie Nelson, Ricky Skaggs, George Strait, and the Judds. Then, as the clock ticked down to the closing, he opened the envelope, peeked inside and grinned, then looked up and announced the winner.

CHAPTER 59

The morning after Reba won the Entertainer of the Year award, she remembers, "I woke up and thought, 'Well, I'm Entertainer of the Year now. Well, that's good.' But it didn't feel like it had changed anything. I'm still me. And I'm still biting at the bit. I still want more, more, more, and better, better, better. You know, better shows, better albums."

Actually, a lot of things had changed. She noticed them first when she went back to Stringtown and into the grocery store. "There was such a commotion I couldn't even remember what I came in there for," she said. "They were lining up for autographs, or they would just stand back and stare and say, 'Oooh, there she is.' It was weird."

Reba tried to convey a simple message: "C'mon, y'all, I'm still Reba. I was just in here a couple weeks ago. Y'all didn't act like that then."

Back at the ranch, she saddled up her horse, Leggs. She had bought the horse from Charlie for three thousand dollars. "He wanted more, but we bartered," said Reba smiling. "He said he got cheated." She rode Leggs out back of their ranch and just spent some time by herself, getting away from it all in the Oklahoma hills at the same time she was trying to let it all soak in a little more gradually.

But she was going to have to get used to a "new" Reba, as evidenced by a concert after she had won the award. It was in Florida and "we was doing everything like we always do," she recalled. "The band went out. The lights went down. The music went off. The emcee went up there, and all of a sudden, the crowd got wilder and louder and louder. And I though, 'Geez, who's out there on that stage?' I thought maybe some big star must've shown up."

But she was the big star. Backstage someone said, "Well, sounds like they're ready for ya!" Her reaction was a quizzical "That's for me? Whew-eeee!"

Then the audience started stomping their feet on the floor and yelling, "Reba, Reba, Reba!" "It freaked me out," said the object of their affection.

And she couldn't help wondering, "Where was all this last week? Do I look different to you?"

She admitted the CMA show had taken its toll on her. "That's about the most stressful thing you can go through," she said about sitting in the audience, nominated for five different awards. "You sit there a nervous wreck all night. Every time one of them came up, it was like my brain went *Yeeeeeee*! I was a basket case by the end of the show."

But one by one, her dreams were all coming true. At the end of the year she received the news she'd have a gold record to hang on the wall: *Whoever's in New England* had sold over half a million units.

CHAPTER 60

In October 1986, when Reba McEntire won Entertainer of the Year, country music was still a man's world, but with some notable differences.

First, the number 1 song that week was held by a woman (Tanya Tucker with "Just Another Love") and four of the top five songs were by women: Crystal Gayle with "Cry" at number 2, Rosanne Cash at number 5 with "Second to No One," and a duet with Anita Pointer and Earl Thomas Conley, "Too Many

Times" at number 4. (Interestingly, this was the first interracial duet ever on the country charts; they performed during the CMA telecast).

All in all, thirty-two entries on the hundred-song Country Singles Chart featured a woman singing. Those singers included Juice Newton, Marie Osmond, Barbara Mandrell, Janie Fricke, Anne Murray, Holly Dunn, Dolly Parton, Kathy Mattea, Judy Rodman, Tammy Wynette, Nicolette Larson, and Lacy J. Dalton; Reba had two entries: "What Am I Gonna Do About You" at number 44, going up the chart, and "Little Rock" at number 64, falling off.

In addition to women singing alone or in duets with men, there were several female groups: Sweethearts of the Rodeo, the Girls Next Door, and the Forrester Sisters, as well as a mother-daughter duo, the Judds, and a father-daughter duo, the Kendalls. Clearly the country music industry was much more open to women than it once had been.

But while women were being *heard* on the radio a-plenty, they were not necessarily being *bought* by consumers in record stores. The singles chart reflects radio airplay, but the album chart reflects album sales. And if a record doesn't sell, it doesn't make money for the label. (Money from airplay goes to songwriters and publishers—not the labels or artists).

On the album charts, only seventeen of the seventy-five positions were held by women. The highest was number seven, by Janie Fricke, followed by the Judds at number 8. In the Top Twenty were six women—including Reba, whose album *Whoever's in New England* was at number 16.

The conclusion: overall, about a third of all country singles heard or all country albums purchased featured female artists. While the figures vary from week to week, the one-third share for women in country music remains pretty constant. (In popular music the proportion is more like 20 percent.) It has certainly held from 1976, when Reba first entered the charts, until 1986, and the trend has continued through the early 1990s.

Who buys country music? Well, men buy a significant amount—and they want male artists. And women buy a significant amount, and they want male artists, too. Actually, sales of country music are pretty evenly split between the sexes.

Of the five most significant artists of the 1980s—Alabama, Ricky Skaggs, Randy Travis, George Strait, and Reba McEntire— only one is female. If you add Ricky Van Shelton the odds get lower. If you put the Judds and Dolly Parton in that group, it helps the odds a little but generally reaffirms the obvious: country music is a man's world and it aims to stay that way.

A conclusion must be drawn: it is a lot easier being a female artist in country music than it used to be, but it still ain't easy. That is perhaps best demonstrated by the winners of the CMA's Entertainer of the Year award, the top honor in country music. Since its inception in 1967, the award has been given to men nineteen times and to women five times. Only four women have ever won the award: Loretta Lynn in 1972, Dolly Parton in 1978, Barbara Mandrell in 1980 and 1981, and Reba McEntire in 1986.

PART 6

ENTERTAINER

OF THE YEAR

CHAPTER *61*

At the beginning of 1987 Reba was in the studio recording two new albums: her regular release, which would come out around September, and a Christmas album.

Winning the Entertainer of the Year award—and with a project appealing to women—had given her a real shot in the arm and a direction to take. It was reflected in her upbeat attitude, growing feminism, and positive thinking as well as the constant touring and working on her career.

Just after the awards she had said that winning CMA Entertainer of the Year was "the best advertising in the world. It's a sky's-the-limit situation. We haven't even started yet."

In February she won her first Grammy, the Country Female Vocal award, for her performance on "Whoever's in New England." But she wasn't there to collect the award in person. "We were real busy and fixin' to go out on a tour the next day," said Reba. "And the award I won wasn't gonna be televised, so I wasn't gonna go."

In April Reba won two awards from the Academy of Country Music: top female vocalist, and top video for "Whoever's in New

England." At the end of the awards show, Reba performed "Sweet Dreams" a capella. Afterward, MCA surprised Reba with her second gold album, this one for *What Am I Gonna Do About You*.

A major reason for her success in selling so many albums? The videos. "They were on HBO—places where people wouldn't normally listen to country music," said Reba. "I was on the video clip right behind Aretha Franklin—pretty good company to be hanging around with. When people are in a hotel room or at home watching a movie and in between movies they run my video, that's great exposure. I think the videos helped a hundred percent."

Also in April she ventured into the restaurant business, opening Reba McEntire's Kitchen on Music Valley Drive, near the Opry House, in Nashville. The restaurant, featuring down-home cooking, was operated by a firm called The Ranch, Inc., which also operated the Loretta Lynn's Kitchen restaurants. There were plans for a major chain.

Through the first half of 1987 Reba continued her grueling pace on the road, performing with her band, the Road Slugs. (Reba coined the name during a long tour when the group was in Kentucky; they had been running late and had to take the stage without any showers.) Life had gotten to be a series of hotel rooms, auditoriums, and long interstate highways. She lived for the spotlight; every night she would walk on the stage, hear the applause, feel the love of the crowd, and perform her show. That hour or so on the stage made it all worthwhile. And now that she was winning major awards and selling gold records, well, she could see that it was all worth it. No sacrifice is too great for a career that lands you on top. And so every night after her show, she climbed back on her bus and let the miles roll away beneath her as she went to the next town to do it all over again.

She reiterated over and over how she liked to stay busy. And her shows had become more elaborate, generally including at least three changes of clothes. Not all reviewers liked what they saw. In a review in Berkeley, California, the reviewer J. Poet noted:

> The show never built up any steam. Reba sings two "easy" tunes, wows us with a couple of notes that could make a bat dizzy, and exits to change clothes while the band jams on Hank Williams or, believe it or not, Duke Ellington and Count Basie. Then the star returns in new duds (jeans, a blue-and-white print dress, etc.) does a number or two from the new LP, belts out another show-stopping hit, and runs back to the dressing room. It was so "professional" and formulaic that you could tell early on any magic that happened would be purely accidental, and the "down-home" patter between songs was so Las Vegas that it made me cringe.

A reviewer in Savannah, Georgia, noted, "The only contrived element seems to be her need to change dresses—the colors were gray, black, and white, if that means anything—three times."

At a concert in May, reviewer Noel Davis wrote, "She did make one mistake in pacing when she grouped three of her saddest songs together and then underscored the point by changing into a black dress for the segment. A cloud of gloom temporarily descended on the amphitheater that sent many patrons scurrying for the relief of the beer concessions."

Some reviewers liked the effect, though. Of a concert in Seattle in May, a reviewer noted, "Toward the end of one particularly gloomy number about divorce, she waited briefly for her crucial cue, and just as it came she glanced down, started to sing the sad words, and—when the tension was at its most excruciating—she reached out absentmindedly and picked a speck of lint off her dress as she let the lyrics pour forth." The

185

reviewer called the gesture "the perfect touch," as it "for a moment brought everything into focus. It was a reassuring reminder that country music remains largely a matter of honest expression, and it left no doubt that McEntire is one of the most magnetic presences in its orbit today."

At Fan Fair in June, Reba appeared at her booth on June 9 at 4 P.M., signing autographs for two hours. Fans had begun lining up at 11:30 A.M. It was a beautiful booth, splashed with colors of rose and black, with an elevated area for Reba to sit. There were flowers, rose-colored vases, and glittering script proclaiming "Reba" and "Entertainer of the Year." The centerpiece was a thirty-by-forty-inch color photo of Reba accepting the 1986 Entertainer of the Year award from the CMA. A handcarved wooden horseshoe framed the photograph, and a pair of large wooden belt buckles, replicas of the one Reba was wearing onstage, flanked the booth like brown beacons. The booth was designed by Cindy Owen, from Jackson, Mississippi, and won first prize in the Fan Fair booth competition.

CHAPTER 62

More and more, Reba was espousing her feminism. In a number of interviews she took the opportunity to be a spokesperson for women in country music. To one reporter at the beginning of 1986 she said, "Women have to prove themselves in any business. Women in country music have more control now, they're more modern in their attitudes. There's also more work, not just openin' shows but closin' 'em, too." She wanted to "sing songs for women and present their story to the public. Not by being sympathetic, but by being on their side.

"I sing songs for women, dress for women. I try not to offend them, so they won't mind their husbands or boyfriends enjoying my shows right along with them. That way the men don't feel uncomfortable either."

To another reporter she talked about her relationship to the women in her audience. "You don't want to feel threatened. You want to be a friend. I know I messed up going out wearing spandex pants and sequined tops and trying to be something I wasn't. I went back to my more comfortable dresses and things women wanted to wear or wanted to see me wear, and I got along with them a lot better."

She added, "I tried to make me into something I wasn't. I wanted to wear sequins and stuff. I wanted to dress fancy-dancy. I wanted sparkles. I always had hand-me-downs when I was a kid."

When compared to Loretta Lynn and other female singers, she said, "I choose songs with a little different attitude toward women. Loretta Lynn and I both sing songs for women, and we sing things that they can't always say to men but would like to. The difference, though, is that back in the Sixties or Seventies Loretta would sing a song like 'Don't Come Home A'Drinkin' With Lovin' on Your Mind,' but nowadays I'll sing a song with a message like, 'Don't even consider coming home, because we're not gonna put up with it any longer.' That's the difference with the Eighties and Nineties women."

But she added, "I do have an old-fashioned streak, too. I do think women should be treated special in some ways. But there shouldn't be limitations, because women can do whatever men can do."

She was also trying to speak for women within the country music community. "I like to use songs written by women whenever possible," she said. "Women have a hard time getting started in this business, and I like to do my little part to make it easier for them. There are lots of doors closed to you just because you're female. I'd like to open some of 'em.

"I try to find songs written by women," she said. "They seem to zero in a little bit more and have that personal touch women can relate to."

To *Nashville Banner* reporter Michael McCall she said, "I really do think it's just as tough for women now as it was when I started. Women still have to struggle, still have to prove themselves four times as much as any man does. The only way you're going to make it is accept that challenge and work that much harder."

Reba told reporter Holly Gleason that she tried to sing songs for women "because it is the women who buy the tickets and the records. They buy the music for the household, so naturally you want to appeal to them. And since I am a woman, I sing about the things that are natural for me. Those themes are all over my records. What I'm singin' for is to sing for those women out there and make 'em realize that they're special.

"First of all, God created them and made them in his likeness. And all of God's creations are special. And secondly, I think that women ought to be treated specially. Women are ladies, they deserve to be treated as such.

"I didn't say there was anything a woman couldn't do. All I was saying is that sometimes they forget how really special they are and that they deserve to be treated nicely."

She found out she was also attracting younger people to her show as well. "At the beginning of my career, I was opening for such acts as Conway Twitty and the Statler Brothers," she said. "There weren't too many teens in the audience at those shows. I started concentrating more on women, and it turns out that songs for women also target teens. Now I have teens at my shows and I get letters from lots of young people. I'm tickled pink about that."

CHAPTER 63

Reba's performances were attracting a lot of attention, especially the obvious emotions she was showing onstage, crying during some of her songs that talked about a relationship ending or a woman facing the dilemma of finding someone new while still attached to her old love.

A highlight in her show continued to be the song "Somebody Should Leave," about a couple that is staying together when they should be splitting. One writer noted, "So convincing is McEntire's performance . . . that fans have written to her expressing sympathy about her troubled marriage, which is not in trouble at all. None of McEntire's material is autobiographical, but she sings it with absolute conviction."

Replied Reba, "I don't just sing it, I get into it." And to another reporter she said, "Mainly, when I'm singing a song, I put myself in that character's position. I'm almost acting in a sense." She had learned the essential key to a great singer: it's not the voice alone, but the emotion it carries; it's not just singing a song, but delivering an emotion.

She was asked about "Only in My Mind," a song she had written about someone telling her mate, when he confronts her about cheating, that she had cheated "only in my mind." Reba explained, "Well, it says in the Bible that if you think it instead of doin' it, it's still a sin. But so many people do come up to me and say, 'Ooooh, that is my song.' You know, we're all guilty of once in a while thinkin' things, although we don't go through and do it." She had said the song came to her while she was in her dressing room one night and she overheard someone asking a person if they'd ever been unfaithful. "I thought about what

President Carter said about being unfaithful in his mind," said Reba.

Of "You're the First Time I've Thought About Leaving," a song where the singer looks longingly at a new love while staying attached to her old lover, Reba admitted, "I get all choked up. It's not exactly acting—not acting at all. It's just that when I have a good song, I know what it's saying. If I don't know, then the listener's not going to know." She explained that it's "almost a cheating song," but the woman decides not to. "A lot of women have told me 'Oh, that's my life. But don't tell my husband.' "

Reba usually explained her emotional performances by saying, "I do pretend or play-act an awful lot when I'm onstage or practicing or sitting in front of a mirror putting on my makeup or listening to demos. I'm quite a pretender."

She did not talk about ranching and rodeoing much, but when she did, she noted, "The best thing I got out of rodeo was traveling and meeting my husband."

A number of writers defended Reba's performances, saying she was an exceptionally good actress in concert and going on to tell how stable her life had been and how happily married she was in actuality. One writer stated: "Unlike the women she sings to and/or about, Reba has been neither dried out, divorced, nor downtrodden. (She has even turned down songs that mention liquor.) She has been married for ten years to Charlie Battles, a former three-time national steer wrestling champion. Battles divides time between the ranch and managing his wife's career. The couple, she says, are very happy."

An interesting story appears here. It seems someone was talking to Minnie Pearl and said Reba must have had a hard life. Minnie replied, "No, not that I know of." "But she's been divorced two or three times," the lady insisted. Then Minnie explained that, although Reba's music had given indications of leading a hard life, she has actually led a very stable life. "But isn't she divorced?" asked the fan. Minnie answered, "No, she has a very happy marriage."

When the story was relayed to Reba, she said, "That was cute;

Minnie Pearl handled it nicely. All it means is that I'm a good actress."

CHAPTER 64

Reba McEntire filed for divorce from Charlie Battles on June 25, 1987—just four days after their eleventh anniversary. The papers were filed in Atoka, Oklahoma, at the Atoka County Courthouse by Tulsa attorney Larry Leonard.

When you go for that big brass ring, the superstardom of the stratosphere, you have to make sacrifices. And one of the first things to get lost is your family.

It's not logical or premeditated, really. And Lord knows there are faults on both sides. But when it comes down to losing the family or losing that big mega-superstardom, the family always goes. It's happened to a lot of folks—some who made it and some who didn't. This may have happened to Reba.

By 1987 Reba and Charlie Battles weren't the same couple they had been when they had married in 1976. Nobody is after ten-plus years. But there were changes bigger than the normal growth of two human beings, bigger than the passing years that wear away at us like the tides until, washing our shorelines away, we are changed to what we never guessed we'd be.

When Reba and Charlie married, he was a champion steer wrestler—a hero on the rodeo circuit—and Reba was a sweet, innocent girl who was filled with ambition but had not much accomplishment to go with it.

By 1987 Charlie was a burly guy who no longer wrestled steers. And Reba was a big star. In 1976 she had been easily awed by everyone and everything. By 1987 people were in awe of her, and she was awed by less and less. At first, Charlie had been the backbone of that family—the star performer—now it was Reba. In 1976 they had become Mr. and Mrs. Charlie Battles; by 1987 they had become Mr. and Mrs. Reba McEntire.

Charlie was tired of traveling, tired of the country music spotlight, tired of having to share Reba with the world. He was forty-two now, and his sons, Lance and Cody, were twenty and sixteen. If he and Reba were going to have kids, now was the time.

For Reba, her career came first: that unquenchable thirst for stardom, that constant striving and clawing for higher and higher mountains. To be bigger than the biggest—when you can see it, you can't turn away. A glimpse is all it takes.

There are signs along the way. There are entertainers who claim to have wonderful marriages and home lives, but are on the road constantly. A number of show-biz marriages have lasted many years because one partner stayed out on the road while the other accepted staying at home. But Reba and Charlie somehow didn't seem to cut a deal like this, although Reba was on the road 275 days in 1986 and would be gone the same amount in 1987. There may not be a lot of harmony at home when somebody is gone that much.

But that's not the whole story.

"Reba got into a religious thing," remembers Charlie Battles. "She was talking in tongues and things I didn't understand. I believe in the good Lord as much as anybody, but that was all beyond me. Anyway, she kept saying this was the Lord's will."

Charlie asked her if she had been unfaithful, "and she swore up and down she hadn't," he said. "I trusted Reba a hundred percent. And in twelve years of marriage, I never cheated on her, never even thought about cheating on her. I worshiped the ground she walked on."

Charlie was baffled about Reba and what was happening in their marriage; from what she told him he thought it all boiled down to God wanting them to get a divorce. A month or so later, Reba came back to gather up her belongings, and Charlie was there. "I told her she could take what was hers," he said.

"She could take her personal stuff. She wanted to take everything."

Reba kept calling to get the divorce settled and over with. Charlie said he kept wanting to sit down with her and talk, but she kept him on the phone. He was adamant about keeping the ranch. "I bought that ranch in 1980, before she had ever hit," he said. "And we kept two separate checking accounts, one for the ranch and one for the music."

The ranch wasn't making them rich, but it was doing well and had always paid for itself. Charlie Battles had worked hard on that ranch; it was his whole life. And so while Reba continued to hit the spotlights all across the country, Charlie spent his time on the ranch, working his horses and cattle.

CHAPTER 65

After filing for divorce, Reba continued touring with a vengeance. Home was on the road; at this point there was literally no "home" to go home to, unless she stayed at her parents' house in Oklahoma or some motel room somewhere else. And so she would stay on the road 275 days in 1987.

Charlie had been her business manager, but right after filing for divorce, Reba named Narvel Blackstock to take Charlie's place. Narvel had started out with her as the steel guitar player, then had become road manager, taking care of the day-to-day cares and concerns of life on the road for Reba.

Shortly after Reba had filed for divorce, Narvel Blackstock filed for divorce from his wife in Burleson, Texas. He had been married at sixteen; the couple had three children.

Charlie says that Reba "wasn't the same girl I'd married. She changed from a little country girl to something else." Charlie says the changes really had begun in 1984, when she won her first CMA Female Vocalist of the Year award, and couldn't be ignored after she won Entertainer of the Year in 1986.

"Nobody ever stays the same," says Charlie Battles with hurt and resignation in his voice. "She used to be real open and friendly, but that stopped. You could see a difference." He says that after the divorce settlement in December—where Charlie got the ranch and Reba got her freedom—they quit speaking.

Reba was on top now and she enjoyed the view. In August she told Jack Hurst, "When it takes you a long time to get somewhere—like walkin' up steps real slow, gettin' to the top of the Empire State Building by going up the stairs—you have a lot of time to think and plan what you want to do when you get there. Once you get there, you think, 'Let's stay up here a little bit and see what we can do.' "

She had decided to move to Nashville, she told Hurst. "I didn't know where else to go. I spend so much time here, I thought, 'Why not make it a base?' " But she quickly added, "The thing I'd like most to do is travel. There are lots of things I want to see and go do. When we travel on business, we just see the hotel, the airport, the highway, or the hall; we don't get to sightsee. So although I've been a lot of places, I've missed a lot."

In September she was in Houston performing. Writer Bob Claypool interviewed her and reviewed her show. He stated, "Oddly enough, the only lags were during the times when McEntire made offstage costume changes while the band vamped through something. Her four different outfits were enough to earn her the title of the 'Loretta Young of Country Music.' " He added, "Apparently, there isn't any kind of music Reba can't sing, but, when she gets her near-operatic range and emotional range and emotional phrasing into a ballad, it will raise chill-bumps on the most blasé listener."

The Last One to Know, which Reba later referred to as her "divorce album," was released in September 1987. Produced by

Jimmy Bowen and Reba, the album begins with the title cut, a song about love ending with questions left hanging. "The Girl Who Has Everything" concerns the old question, What kind of wedding gift do you give the woman who's got your man? In the poignant "Just Across the Rio Grande" illegal immigrants, trapped in poverty because they were born on the wrong side of the river, look at the land of plenty.

"I Don't Want to Mention Any Names" is an up-tempo, western swing number where the singer needs to discuss the intentions of another woman who's got eyes on her man. In the closing song on side 1, "Someone Else," the singer denies there's another man in her life.

Side 2 opens with "What You Gonna Do About Me," a ballad about breaking up and splitting up possessions—and having to face the turmoil that puts a small child through. "I Don't Want to Be Alone," written by Reba, begins in a minor key, with a Bobbi Gentry feel. The singer doesn't like being alone and doesn't want to stay that way, but she's worried about letting the object of her affection know her feelings. She wants to make a pass but doesn't want to get passed over, so she's nervous about making the first move.

"The Stairs" tells the story of a battered wife, trapped in a bad marriage with an alcoholic partner, who covers up and pretends she fell down the stairs when her husband hits her. "Love Will Find Its Way to You" is a joyous number about a girl who is alone but has hope: open up your heart and there's someone waiting just for you. The album closes with "I've Still Got the Love We Made"; mementos and other material objects may be lost, but something intangible still remains.

After the album came out, Reba began doing interviews again. She announced she was moving to Nashville; she had leased a house near Radnor Lake. But on the road, at her concerts, she seemed to be avoiding her fans, going straight from her bus to the stage and back again. She must have known they all wanted to ask the same question, to hear about the divorce. And Reba was apparently just not ready to discuss that—especially with strangers, no matter how well they knew her.

To reporters, she talked about several songs on her new album. Reba said she went to Jimmy Bowen and "I told him I wanted to put ['The stairs'] on the album. He said, 'You're stickin' your neck out.' And I said, 'Well, it's gotta be said,' If there's a woman out there who's being abused and I sing about it, maybe that will open a door for her or take down a wall so that she can see that she needs to talk to somebody about this. Maybe this will help her."

The inclusion of "The Stairs" on the album led some writers to incorrectly speculate that Charlie Battles had abused her. Both Reba and Charlie emphatically say these rumors were unjustified.

Of "Just Across the Rio Grande" Reba said, "The first time I heard it, it touched my heart. I don't know their [Mexicans'] situation, but I do know America, and we take things for granted so bad it's pathetic—freedom, food, junk food. Anybody can get anything instantly without waiting and worrying about tomorrow. The line that got me was 'He heard they ate three meals a day across the Rio Grande.' That made me open my eyes a lot."

She also said, "I don't think we've tapped into exactly what we're supposed to be doing. I've always known that we're going to be doing something that nobody else has done in country music. It hasn't been shown to me what yet, but I'm confident it will be."

The CMA Awards show was coming round again, and reporters asked her about winning the Entertainer of the Year honors a second time. "That would be incredible," she exclaimed. "But I'm just delighted to get nominated again. It won't devastate us if we don't win. I'm standin' firm, and my career is not based on awards, anyway. I don't want to say that it doesn't make a difference, because it does—it gets you a lot of publicity and it's a real boost to your career. But I don't work with awards in mind, never have—you can't work that way."

A reporter in Texas asked her about the divorce. "It was just one of those things," she said. "Can't be helped."

Was there any big scandal or tabloid stuff, he inquired? "Oh no, nothing like that," said Reba. "It just happened. It's friendly and all."

That was the final word on that subject.

Reba did say she did not like being insulated from the public. "I couldn't live like that," she said. "I just couldn't. I've got to get out, be with other people, and I still do. I still love to go to Wal-Mart and do my shopping. Do I get recognized? Oh, sure. Sometimes I have to spend quite a bit of time giving autographs in places like that, but it's worth it, I don't mind. After they see I'm just another person, they say, 'Thanks, have a good time shopping,' and they go off. It's real neat—my fans have always been like that.

"I think if you hide from your fans, then they really seek you out. But if you're open with them from the start, they just love you for it and they respect you. I don't have any problems with it at all. Havin' to hide yourself away, that's just scary. I'd quit the business if I had to do that—after all, I want to enjoy my career, and I'm not gonna be a prisoner."

To another reporter she said she liked touring "because I get to see different parts of the country. I saw Mount Rushmore, beautiful California, Valley Forge, and not long ago we went to Chicago where there was a jazz and blues festival. If I wasn't in music, I would have never been to all those places. I enjoy traveling all over the country."

She said she "doesn't think about crossing over to pop much; it just doesn't bother me. I think that has a lot to do with the song, the way 'Lucille' crossed over. If that happens to me, great, but I still love country music most of all. It's what I sing."

When asked about her being a hero to new, young female country singers, Reba replied, "That's nice to know, really. It's nice to know you're being listened to by people like that and that you might have some influence or something. I love all those young traditional people—I think the young blood that's coming into country music now is one of the best things that's happened to it for years. They're talented and they've got confidence. They're going to make a difference."

She did admit she missed cooking in the kitchen. "When I'm at home, I spend a lot of time in the kitchen preparing my favorite stuff," she said. "Baked beans, cole slaw, red beans, cornbread, fried potatoes—nothing too fattening!"

And, of course, she was still immersed in her show, her image, and her audience. "I like to show personality," she said about performing. "I want people to have fun. I constantly want to improve on my performances and make sure they're not boring. I don't want any dead spots in the show. Sometimes my audiences range from rowdy to blah. In Canada and the Northwest, the people are reserved and polite. They sit back and listen; I actually like that.

"I'm happy with the gradual success I've had. I had a lot to learn about the business, and I had a lot of good teachers. There are some people who become successful so fast, but I like it this way better.

"All this attention feels real good. And I thank God for a lot of that. Things are rolling right along now, and we're sure not stoppin'. We worked hard for twelve years, and this is the payoff."

She said her singing was "a God-given gift. I can't find a better explanation than that. Of course, it takes lots of practice. Hearing how you want it to sound in your head and doing it that way are two different things. I just like to experiment with range."

She said that she was an everyday person. "That's what we all are, regardless. We're all out there looking for the same basic things, so that puts us all in the same boat together, doesn't it? I'm basically just a working girl myself."

She admitted she had recently canceled a European tour "because management thought I had more important things to tend to stateside right now."

At the end of 1987, when one reporter asked how she was feeling, Reba replied, "One hundred percent, full-fledged, all the way."

CHAPTER 66

At the Country Music Association Awards show, Reba won the Female Vocalist of the Year award for the fourth consecutive year—topping Loretta Lynn and Tammy Wynette, who had each won it three times. But she did not win the Entertainer of the Year honor; Barbara Mandrell was the only female to have done that twice. In 1987 the Entertainer of the Year trophy went to Hank Williams, Jr.

Carrying home her award, Reba set out into the night and did not participate in the news conference after the televised CMA Awards. At this time she was doing a precarious balancing act within the country music community between being high profile and laying low.

The big event in fall 1987 was an appearance at Carnegie Hall in New York on October 28. This would cap off a tour of the Northeast. It would also be her chance to blitz the New York media.

In New York, she continued to espouse the role of women, telling one reporter, "I don't like to be referred to as a 'gal' or a 'chick' or a 'broad.' I am a working woman. I think women do need to be strong. A woman is a very affectionate, intimate, feeling, caring, warm-hearted person. But my mother is one of the strongest people I've ever met in my life. She can cry right along with you at the saddest movie or the most heartbreaking moment. But by durn, when the stress and tension is there, she's the backbone."

When asked about her divorce, Reba replied, "It worked out real fine for a long time until I was kinda asked to come home and stay home and slow down. I worked so hard and so long to get where I am now that I didn't want to slow down. For so many years, Charlie was so supportive, and then it kinda wasn't the most important thing to him. This is my life out here, the music business. I love what I'm doing. When you're out on the road all the time, the family is the people that's out on the road with you."

She talked about being home just before she had finally decided on the divorce, saying, "I would unload the bus, work on the books, I would do anything in the world to keep from sitting and watching TV with Charlie. I couldn't stand it. He'd say, 'Reba, sit down.' And I'd sit down for about ten minutes. The next commercial break, I'd be at it again. I wouldn't care if I was rearranging the closet."

To another reporter, she explained the reason for the divorce was that she was "restless."

Later, she said, "When I was married, I was very insecure. I needed support and Charlie was very supportive. But I was learning all this time. I would want to do things a certain way and it was taking a long time to get it done. When you're a wife, you have to convince"—she paused for a moment—"you have to be careful how you say things." Then she continued, "It got to the point where the things I wanted to do were being taken away from me." But now, she said, "I'm single and I'm fine," adding that "The people I have around me—my band and my crew—are my second family."

Earlier in the year, when asked to describe herself, she said she was "very spunky, outgoing, kind of stubborn, willful. I don't like for people to say, 'You can't do this and you can't do that.' Whenever they tell me that, I prove 'em wrong." She added, "If I get my mind set on something, I go at it." And that summed her up throughout 1987.

In the interviews before the Carnegie Hall appearance, Reba was clearly nervous about playing for the New York audience. "After you've been shopping there and seen Broadway plays, you know there's a different kind of people up there," she said. "They're used to sophisticated entertainment. My band and crew and I are more excited about this than any other place because we've heard about it all our lives."

Discussing the early years of her career, Reba told *New York Times* reporter Stephen Holden, "When I first started out in country, we were 'girl singers' who were told what to sing. I heard many horror stories about women who were told to keep quiet in the studio. At around the time I decided to have more control over my material, the trend in Nashville was to write 'fluffy' tunes that weren't at all like the music I had grown up listening to. I had to go to the writers and ask them to write the kind of songs I wanted."

About crossing over, she said, "I think it would be a huge mistake to consciously try for that. It's like planning a good time on your day off."

It is some milestone of sorts when performers begin referring to themselves in the third person. Somehow they begin looking at their public persona as something different from their private self. Reba was doing this now trying to explain her songs. "I don't sing country," she said, "I don't sing pop. I just sing Reba songs."

By the time she got to New York, she had been playing a number of concerts in the Northeast and felt much more comfortable with those audiences. "I don't know who started the rumor that nobody likes country music up here," she observed. "But I'd like to stop it quick because it's definitely wrong. We've played in New Jersey, Long Island, Massachusetts, Vermont, and Maine, and they've all been sellouts or close-to's. And I can't believe the enthusiasm of the people who come out. We were in Massachusetts the other night and people came from Connecticut and New York, and some of them had followed us from state to state. There's really a huge following for country music in this area."

Attorney and manager Bill Carter was excited about the overwhelming response she had received in New York. "There was a lot of risk in coming here," he said. "A lot of people in Nashville, a lot of people everywhere, warned me not to try a concert here. But we deliberately did not play here for the last five years. We felt when we came in we wanted it to be a prestige event."

The Carnegie Hall appearance was an astounding success and New Yorkers were quite taken with Reba. *New York Post* writer Dan Aquilante wrote, "Although it wasn't quite the Grand Ole Opry, the sweetheart of the rodeo and the reigning Queen of Country Music, Reba McEntire's New York debut at Carnegie Hall was stunning."

Wayne Robbins of *Newsday* wrote, "This sure isn't the Dew Drop Inn," adding, "There was none of the effusive 'Golly, jee-pers gee whiz, look-at-li'l-ol'-me-in-New York' asides that country singers usually bring to a show in the big city," before closing with, "While she remains strongly part of a country tradition, McEntire's vocal prowess and stage command at one point made one think of a rodeo version of Lena Horne."

At the end of her concert, Reba received a five-minute standing ovation. As one music industry insider observed, "Even the Pope didn't get a standing ovation in New York."

CHAPTER *67*

In 1988 Reba was living the contemporary version of the single life, building a business empire with herself atop a huge organization in Nashville. She had climbed to the top of country music as a female entertainer; now she was aiming for the top as a female executive and entrepreneur.

Reba had purchased a building in Nashville in February, right across from the state fairgrounds where the annual Fan Fair get-together is held, and established her own management firm. She had also started a publishing company, began promoting some of her own concerts, and generally moved most of the decision-making in-house. This often happens when an artist reaches superstar status: they yearn for control and create an umbrella organization for all their career activities. It is the music industry's version of a "cottage industry," and Reba made this move in 1988.

It was a good time for building in country music. After the boom years in the early 1980s when the urban-cowboy craze had boosted sales of country music to around $250 million, a big crash occurred as overall sales plummeted to $175 million. This came about because country music executives tried to sell "country pop" or "countrypolitan" music, a watered-down version of country music, to their audiences. But the audiences didn't buy it.

Thank goodness the executives on Music Row finally read the handwriting on the wall—first with the success of Ricky Skaggs, then with the success of George Strait, and began signing acts who played traditional country music. Reba McEntire's success with *My Kind of Country* was also fuel to the flame, and then Randy Travis hit like an explosion. The fast train from Carolina scored major sales and media exposure beginning in 1986, and from this time on, only a fool would deny that real country fans wanted real country music. This opened the doors for acts such as Ricky Van Shelton, Clint Black, Garth Brooks, Alan Jackson, and others—the second wave of new traditionalists.

By this time Reba was firmly in place as the top female artist in country music. And her success opened the doors for acts such as Shelby Lynn and Patty Loveless. There was even an increased demand to see and hear some old-timers like Loretta Lynn and Tammy Wynette.

Ironically, as traditional country music was storming through the industry like a giant locomotive, Reba elected to record some very nontraditional country songs for her album *Reba*.

"I wanted to try some torch songs," she said, "because we'd had some success doing 'Since I Fell for You' in our live show.

We did it at Carnegie Hall, and the New York critics just went nuts about it—gave us real good reviews. So we put 'Sunday Kind of Love' on the album."

In fact, the Carnegie Hall appearance, and the tremendous reception of Reba's version of the old Lenny Dee classic, "Since I Fell for You," prompted Bruce Hinton, head of marketing for MCA Records in Nashville, to strongly encourage Reba to do a whole album of songs like this. "It's the only way you'll broaden your audience," he told her.

She had put the old Aretha Franklin classic "Respect" on her album, too. People were curious about why she did it, and she answered, "I was gonna do it to open my show, because I thought the women would really like it—you know, we want respect, give us respect, and all that. Jimmy Bowen said, 'Well, why don't you put it on the album?' I didn't expect that, but we did."

In doing the *Reba* album, Reba had said, "What's good about being in the country music field is that the spectrum is so broad. On one end, you've got traditional going into bluegrass, and on the other end it's almost pop. Country music gives you the greatest freedom of all."

She admitted the *Reba* album "was a departure from the straight-ahead traditional music I've been doing—but I just wanted to do something different. It was a challenge to me. I'm not leaving traditional country music. I'm not going to leave my country roots. When writers bring songs to me, we sit down and decide whether to put steel or fiddle on them. This album just didn't lend itself to that."

The album kicks off with "So, So, So Long," with Reba moaning before kicking into an up-tempo positive love song that wants love to go on forever and ever and ever. "Sunday Kind of Love," which was a hit for Jo Stafford in 1947, has a smoky, bluesy, 1940s nightclub feel as the singer wishfully yearns for that perfect kind of love.

The modern-day dilemma of someone playing the dating game after she thought those days were long over and gone is the predicament in "New Fool at an Old Game." "You're the One

I Dream About" mourns lost opportunities with someone who came along one promise too late. Side 1 closes with "Silly Me," a ballad that opens with just Reba and a piano as she sings about falling in love with an old friend when she should've known better; she's been hurt before by love and didn't want it to happen again—but the nights do get cold when you sleep alone.

"Respect," the classic rhythm and blues song written and first recorded by Otis Redding, begins side 2, and Reba is sassy belting out this anthem for the downtrodden. The singer asks her lover to treat her right and make forever last that long in "Do Right by Me." "I Know How He Feels" portrays the singer running into her old love with his new lover. And it hurts: it's hard to just give up your old love, no matter how justified.

"Wish I Were Only Lonely" is another bluesy number where the singer faces the dilemma of being lonely for only one special one. The album's closer, "Everytime You Touch Her," has the singer wondering about the new woman in her ex's life. And she has a simple request: she wants her old lover to think about her instead of his new love during their most tender moments.

CHAPTER 68

There wasn't a fiddle or steel guitar on the *Reba* album, nor was there a western shuffle or honky-tonk number. Reba caught some flak for this latest venture and noted, "When those two songs ["Respect" and "Sunday Kind of Love"] came out, some people were offended. They said, 'Well, Reba's leaving country music,' and I said, 'Really? Come on, listen to the way I talk.'"

But, in a way, she understood the fan's reaction. "People like familiarity," she mused. "And when someone steps out of that, it's a shock for them. But I can't do the same thing over and over. It limits my growth. It gets stale. And when that happens,

I get bored. I like to do new things, so people'll say, 'Well, what's she gonna do next?' "

Actually, Reba admitted, "There's a fear in everything I do. If you step out one inch, there's a fear of criticism. So I had to sit down and think, is the criticism worth gambling a career break or a chance to stay in the business longer?" Her biggest worry was "alienating some of my country fans." But, finally, "I had to go with my gut feelings and hope that they liked my singing, regardless of *what* I was singing."

She must have had second thoughts along the way when the criticism came rolling in, especially over her recording and performing "Respect." Primarily, the criticism centered on her singing another woman's song; in this case Aretha Franklin's signature song. "Look, I cut 'Sweet Dreams,' which is Patsy Cline's signature song, and nobody seemed to mind," answered Reba. "In fact, that was one of the things that got a lot of people talking about Reba McEntire. So I really don't understand what all the fuss is about with 'Respect.' Sure, it's Aretha Franklin's signature song, but I don't think that makes it exclusively hers, just like 'Sweet Dreams' isn't exclusively Patsy Cline's. To me, it's about respecting the song."

One reviewer noted that during one performance she "often seemed more concerned with putting on a snazzy show than effectively delivering her material." He added that "McEntire strutted the stage to distraction, punctuated her songs with an assortment of self-conscious gestures and movements aimed at dramatizing the lyrics, and often ended songs caught in a single spotlight in affected, Vegas-like poses."

Another reporter, noting the addition of "Respect" and "Sunday Kind of Love" in her shows, said, "She carried the songs well, but I don't think the tunes were quite what the audience wanted to hear." This reviewer concluded, "McEntire should sit in the audience and watch her opening acts. She boasts about being part of the 'New Traditionalists' movement. Her slick show and prima-donna attitude were more in the ilk of the 'New Capitalist' genre than anything else."

But Reba continued to build an elaborate, flashy show and defended her moves. "Basically, what's happening is I'm broadening my audience," she said. "I don't like to be called a 'traditionalist.' If a person doesn't like to listen to traditional music, he turns off the radio when they say, 'Here's Reba McEntire, traditional singer.' They don't give me a chance. If I'm just a singer, hopefully a good singer with good songs, people will listen to me regardless of the label and hopefully go buy my albums and come to my shows."

She admitted she had been to concerts of pop acts George Michael, Gloria Estefan, Diana Ross, and Lionel Richie. And she wanted to compete with them. "We did our own survey and found out twenty-five percent of people who listen to country only listen to country," explained Reba. "The other seventy-five percent listen to other kinds of music, too. That basically means I'm in competition with George Michael and Michael Jackson and Tiffany. That's why I pay so much attention to what's going on in music. I want to improve my show every year to broaden my audience and get my shows up to the standards younger people expect."

She also said, "I love to listen to black artists sing; they've got so much freedom in their voice. For instance, from listening to Whitney Houston I thought, 'I've got to find some songs with more range in 'em because I can hit higher notes than what I'm doin'.'"

She also liked the idea of doing a flashy show, wearing campy clothes like leather pants and a purple top. "When I walk through that curtain singing 'Respect,' I think I've shocked them," she said. "But to me, that's entertainment. Take them up, take them down. Make them laugh, make them cry." She admitted her elaborate lighting system "cost me a fortune," but she "wanted to be up there with the big boys."

She was certainly doing something right. By 1988 she had four Gold albums and was selling out five-thousand- to ten-thousand-seat halls.

CHAPTER 69

But in spite of all the success, this must have been a perplexing time for Reba, and she confessed, "I miss my family."

She had been performing "I'm a New Fool at an Old Game" and admitted, "It's kind of an encouraging word to people who are starting dating all over again." But, she quickly added, she had been "so busy" that she didn't have time "for any of that social activity stuff."

Although she wasn't "dating," she was spending a lot of time with Narvel Blackstock. Being on the road so much, it gets hard to relate to anyone outside your traveling circle. The people you travel with become your closest friends. It was a time of some big transitions for Reba; she was trying to find a new self and somehow remain her old self.

It must have been difficult for Reba to explain the divorce with Charlie. Ever since she had been getting national attention as a recording artist, she had had a rather public marriage and had pledged undying love for Charlie Battles to her fans, thanking her lucky stars she had such a good marriage. She was totally against divorce for years, and now here she was divorced. She must have found herself in an awkward position, especially now that she was a big star. Big stars are supposed to be happy and secure and contented.

She and Narvel had been on the road since 1980. Narvel's job as road manager was to make sure the singer stays happy and the whole band and crew get from one place to the next. He was the one person who was *there* more than any other.

Reba sought to separate her private from her professional life. People had asked her, "Do you go through everything that you sing about?" and she had replied, "No, the songwriters do that.

"I play-like when I'm writing songs," she said. "It's all pretend; it's all play-like. You write a better song that way."

She admitted, "I thought when I got divorced some songs would come out of it, but none did, so I guess it wasn't meant to be talked about."

She told writer Tommy Goldsmith, "I'm fine; I'm great; I'm happier than I've been in a long time. I just want to be happy. That's my biggest goal—and to do what I'm supposed to do. I know there's something big out there I'm supposed to be doing."

She was proud of her success and enjoying some of its privileges. "I just got my foot in the door where we can do things to help others," she said. "That's what success means. You've got the clout to help other people. We're also at the point where we can go into television and motion pictures and broaden out our audiences and take a few more chances on our shows and albums.

"We're not through yet by any means. "People ask me, 'Are you ready to quit and go home?' and I say, 'Absolutely not! We're kind of just kicking it into second gear.'

"I love to sing; I'm craving it. When I get ready to slow down, that's when I'll slow down. Now that I've got clout to get people's attention, I'm really going to watch who I represent and what spots I do."

She had done an antidrug spot for Nancy Reagan. "I went through about twenty pages of 'em and selected only the one that I could talk about. I've never used drugs. I don't know anything about 'em. If I said, 'Don't use drugs,' those kids'd say, 'How do you know?' I picked one that asked parents just to get down and talk to their kids about it."

She also had a few inner revelations. First, she said, "I need more communication with my family, with the people I work with, and with the fans. That's just basically getting down and talking instead of watching TV." Next, she had learned an age-old lesson: "Money, I've found out, isn't that great a thing," she said. "You can be just as miserable with money as when you are dirt poor. And I've been dirt poor."

But she did have some fun this year, too. On Halloween, she was in Moncton, New Brunswick, with her crew. They had the night off—they had gotten there a day early for their performance—so she threw a Halloween party for her road gang. "We had a real good time," she remembers. "Everybody took a lot of time to get real dressed up. I was the old lady from 'Laugh-In'—Ruth Buzzi. It was a riot. I got to take my frustrations out on everybody, hitting them with my purse all night. We'd been doing shows about five days straight, and on my only day off I had to do press in Toronto—four TV interviews and two newspapers. So I was ready for a nice day off."

In October, at the 1988 Country Music Association Awards show, Reba's reign as Female Vocalist of the Year ended; K. T. Oslin won the award. As a matter of fact, Reba didn't win a single trophy that year.

Actually, she was sort of relieved in a way. "I love winnin', don't get me wrong," she said, "but after winnin' it four times in a row, I felt it was high time for someone else. If I'd won it again, some people would've gone, 'Gimme a break.' I kinda would have felt that way myself."

CHAPTER 70

On June 3, 1989, Reba took her fans by surprise when she married Narvel Blackstock. In fact, she didn't even announce the wedding to her fans until two days afterward.

The wedding—Reba wore a long white dress, carried a spray of exotic orchids, and tucked a penny in her shoe for good luck—took place in the middle of Lake Tahoe on a boat called *The Woodwind*.

Reba had flown in about twenty family members for the ceremony, which took place on a chilly day under threatening skies. The twenty-minute ceremony was performed by Rev. Dan Collier as the boat took a four-and-a-half-hour cruise.

After the ceremony, the guests enjoyed a buffet of cold seafood and champagne. Many of the guests wrapped themselves in blankets to ward off the chill of the fifty-degree weather.

Reba and Narvel had purchased a beautiful estate of about thirty acres with an antebellum-style mansion in January. They could look out their front window and see the Cumberland River rolling by. A board fence rings the mansion, which cost over a million dollars; a long driveway leads up to the home, surrounded by trees. In the best southern tradition, Reba was now living the life of a country music queen and true southern belle.

She and Narvel had been talking about marriage for quite a while, and Reba vowed this marriage would be more private. "My first marriage was about as public as you can get," she said. "So I vowed that when Narvel and I got married we'd do it as quietly as possible."

Reba's mother, Jackie, said, "Reba and Narvel have wanted to get married for some time, but whenever they decided on a date, something unexpected would come up. The timing now is just perfect. Reba feels ready to balance her career—and also have children." It was no secret to those closest to her that Reba wanted a family.

Jackie added that "Reba was the happiest I've ever seen her. She looked like a fairy-tale princess, and Narvel looked so handsome."

The wedding took place on the same day Reba had two shows scheduled. She got married, did a show, held a reception, then did another show before the day was over.

Reba was calling the shots in her career now, but admitted she wasn't doing it alone. "It's not like I'm doing everything myself," she said. "I've got a really great team working with me, and whenever there's a big decision to make, I talk to my booking agent and my publicist and my record company. I get a lot of input, and then I try to make the best decision I possibly can.

"I think as long as you've got new challenges, you're gonna be happy. That's one of the reasons doin' my own management is so exciting. It's a challenge, but it's also givin' me the opportunity to extend what I do creatively with my records into my entire career."

Reba was definitely her own woman. She said, "Now I'll be shapin' my career and makin' my own decisions. In some ways, I feel like I'm comin' into my own, and I can't wait to dig in there. Of course, as I said before, I've got a real good group of people advisin' me, so I couldn't feel better about my situation."

Reba was still concerned about the role of women in the music industry, using her platform to promote the idea that women can compete well in a man's world, in spite of some obvious barriers and drawbacks. "There's never a time I can foresee that women will stop havin' to work hard to achieve what they want to do," observed Reba. "You can't do what you want to do in life by sittin' at home and tellin' your neighbor what you want to do. You have to get out there and prove to the world you can do it."

She noted that women always have to work harder for success than men. "Men even agree with this," she said. "It's not something like, 'whine, whine, whine, we're the females and bless our hearts.' It's not that at all. But it's not on an equal level. Women have to prove themselves capable."

She certainly knew the importance of women in the marketplace. "I don't think people realize this," she observed, "but women buy almost all of the music for the house. They're the ones who buy the concert tickets. If they're the people who are out there doing that, how come nobody seems to be making music for them? I didn't think it was right or fair. So, I set out to try and make music that would be for the women first."

She had gone through a lot of changes in clothes, and was again at the point where she wanted to perform in flashy clothes.

"I'd be dressed in boots, jeans, and a western shirt," she said. "And a woman would say, 'I got more dressed up to come to your show than you did.' That made me want to do more, put on a fancier show, make it worthwhile for people to pay good money to see me."

She added that as a performer, "a woman's gotta do more. She's gotta dazzle more, do more steps and—most of all—she's got to win the women over!"

From Reba's mansion on the Cumberland River near Gallatin, Tennessee, to Nashville's Music Row is about thirty-three miles.

On a wet, windy morning early in 1991, workers are busy adding on to some horse stables. In front of the home, little Shelby Blackstock can see a bay horse grazing. And on cable TV, he can watch some old cowboy shows.

A swimming pool company is working on putting in a pool while Reba is busy fielding phone calls. Her last six albums have all been gold or platinum, her concerts are sold out, and she is in demand with the media. She is planning a new album, doing interviews and photo layouts for major magazines, appearing on key TV shows, and looking for more opportunities in the movies.

Around nine-thirty she and Narvel will get into their BMW and head into their office on Music Row, arriving around ten for meetings, plans, and more phone calls.

Reba is clearly at the top. She stays busy turning down offers for various things, the supreme irony for someone who has arrived at the top of her field after years of trying to get offers and attention. Her awards, her success, her ringing phone and her home—which looks like the home of a country music star *should* look—all attest to Reba's position as the top female singer in country music.

Meanwhile, on this same day back at the ranch in Stringtown, Oklahoma, Charlie Battles is getting into his pickup truck to drive a couple of miles over to Clark and Jackie McEntire's. He's helping Clark move some horses from one pasture to another. In a few days, he'll be heading out to some rodeo. He's a stock contractor now, supplying cattle and horses for rodeo performers.

Charlie says he's doing fine; he hits about forty or fifty rodeos a year now. The last time he saw Reba was at the National Rodeo Finals in Las Vegas at the end of 1990, when she was onstage singing while he was trying to calm a jumpy horse. She never saw him and didn't even know he was there.

She never calls or comes by when she visits her parents, but he still sees her picture in the paper now and then. And he still hears her singing on the radio.

> *Just remember the Red River Valley*
> *And the cowboy who loved you so true...*

On Friday night, March 15, 1991, Reba and her band performed at a private concert before IBM employees in San Diego, California. These are not your ordinary concerts; these are given to a select audience of company people and paid for by the company. But the audience was enthusiastic and the show went well.

The biggest problem for this gig was that Reba and her group had a concert appearance in Fort Wayne, Indiana, the next night. Reba and Narvel always flew in their private jet, a seven-seat Sabre Liner with a bathroom. Normally, the rest of the group all traveled together on buses unless they had to fly; then they would travel on a sixteen-passenger plane booked by Prestige Tours out of Dallas. That plane, however, was being serviced on Saturday, so other arrangements had to be made to fly the group across the country.

Reba and Narvel chartered two smaller jets from Prestige Tours for the group to fly from Brown Field in Otay, California—about fifteen miles southeast of San Diego and four miles north of the Mexican border—to take the group to Fort Wayne. After the concert, the entourage headed out to the field and at about 1:45 in the early morning were ready to fly through the night to Indiana.

Since the whole group could not fit into one plane, they had to be divided. The first group to board the ten-passenger Hawker Siddeley twin-engine jet was most of the band: keyboardist and band leader Kirk Cappello, background singer Paula Kaye Evans, guitarist Michael Thomas, bass player Terry Jackson, keyboard player Joey Cigainero, drummer Tony Saputo, and acoustic guitarist, fiddler, background singer Chris Austin, and road manager Jim Hammon. Then the crew—Captain Don Holms and First Officer Chris Hollinger—taxied down the runway and the group took off. Moments later a wing of the plane apparently clipped the side of the mountain and cartwheeled across the mountainside, exploding before it came to a burnt, twisted stop. Everybody on board was dead.

The second plane, carrying two other band members, saxophonist Joe McGlohon and steel guitarist Pete Finney, took off right after the first plane. When they were airborne, the pilot learned on the radio that the first plane had crashed, but he let the band members rest until they landed in Memphis. McGlohon and Finney thought they were heading straight to Indiana; it was not until they landed that the pilot told them there had been an accident with the first plane, and things did not look good. The pilot then advised them to call their families to tell them they were all right before flying on to Nashville. In Nashville, they heard on the radio that the other plane had crashed and all their cohorts in the band had died.

Meanwhile, back in San Diego, Reba and Narvel were still in their hotel room when the planes had taken off. The pilots for their private jet, Roger and Wayne Woolsey, had been at the airport when the planes took off and knew about the crash, so they had called the hotel and told Narvel the situation. Narvel and Reba stayed at the hotel that night and flew back to Nashville the next day.

News of the disaster reached Nashville and the rest of the world on Saturday morning, March 16, about six hours after the fatal crash. That evening in Nashville, the Nashville Songwriters Association Awards banquet was held at Vanderbilt Plaza Hotel. The tragedy cast a pall over the entire evening.

"I cried all morning," said Kathy Mattea at the awards show, where her husband, Jon Vezner, was named top songwriter for penning the song "Where've You Been." "It's all of our worst nightmares come true. We think about it every time we fly." She added, "Your band is absolutely like family."

K. T. Oslin echoed these sentiments. Band members "literally become your family and in some ways are more than your family," she said. "You depend on them. You travel and eat and go through things together. Oh God, it's so awful."

That night the songwriter ceremonies began with the tape of a song written by Chris Austin, one of those killed in the crash. The song was "We Take a Lot of Memories When We Go" and was cowritten with Jim Rushing. Austin was a talented writer and performer and had been signed to Warner Brothers publishing and Warner Brothers Records for an individual career. He and his wife had been scheduled to sign the papers closing on a home the following week.

When Reba arrived in Nashville on Saturday, she went directly to see Debbie Hammon, wife of her road manager Jim Hammon. She then called families of the band members and other friends. It was a difficult time for her; her publicist announced she was refusing all interviews with the media.

Reba found solace in Psalm 91:

He will cover you with his feathers,
and under his wings you will find refuge;
his faithfulness will be your shield and rampart . . .
A thousand may fall at your side,
ten thousand at your right hand,
but it will not come near you . . .
If you make the Most High your dwelling . . .

then no harm will befall you,
no disaster will come near your tent
For he will command his angels
concerning you
to guard you in all your ways.

On Wednesday, March 20, a memorial service was held for the group at Christ Church on Old Hickory Boulevard. About one thousand were there—singers, musicians, stars, friends, and family—to pay tribute.

At the service, Tanya Goodman Sykes sang several songs, as did the choir, while Dan Scott and L. H. Hardwick—both ministers at the church—delivered a message. But it was the message delivered by Johnny Cash that seemed to have the greatest impact.

First, Cash began with a song, the old Eddy Arnold number "Jim, I Wore a Tie Today," and added the names of the musicians who had died. Then he told of how he had not wanted to come to this service—exactly one week before he was at the funeral service of his mother—but had come anyway. And then he related a story that all traveling musicians and singers understand. Two days after his mother's funeral, Johnny Cash had to perform a concert. And he spoke of talking with Willie Nelson and Nelson relating that the day after his mother was buried, he had to perform a concert.

Reba had canceled several upcoming concerts after the tragedy. But she had been scheduled to perform on the Academy Awards telecast on Monday, March 25, in Los Angeles. She had been looking forward to this performance for a long time; she would perform "I'm Checkin' Out" from the film *Postcards From the Edge.* When she met with her staff on Monday morning, after the tragedy, she announced she would keep that committment.

And so she flew out to Los Angeles and appeared on the Academy Awards, nine days after the tragic plane crash and three days before her thirty-sixth birthday.

As usual, Nashville and the country music community pull together in times of trial and trouble. Many volunteer help, support, and sympathy. An account was set up at a local bank for donations for a fund for the musicians' families. And some artists—Merle Haggard, Sawyer Brown, Kathy Mattea, Janie Fricke—donated proceeds from a series of weekend concerts after the accident to aid the musicians' families. People from Reba's organization were already on the phone rescheduling commitments and deciding which media to talk with—her first interview was with *People* magazine, timed to hit the newstands right after her performance on national television—and planning future shows and commitments.

When you're a public figure, you owe an allegiance to the public. When you're a performer, then you must perform. When you are in the public spotlight, you must face the crowd. When others look to you, you must be strong and go forward. And when you are an entertainer, the show must go on.

Reba's shows go on with a new band. Though the memory of those who died is painful and haunting, she still has her audience of fans who love her and share her life amidst all the heartaches as well as good times. And, at the end of her performances, Reba will get back on a jet that hums through the night. And she will try to catch some rest while the miles flash beneath her, zooming past the moon that hangs like a shiny silver dollar in the American sky.

POSTSCRIPT TO THE PAPERBACK EDITION

1

Three years after the fatal crash, Reba was doing what she always does: performing concerts, pushing projects and promoting her career. At this point she had thirteen Gold albums, eight Platinum, and four Double Platinum albums to her credit. In 1991 she won awards from the American Music Awards and the Academy of Country Music, in 1992 she won two awards from the Academy of Country Music, and in 1993 she was honored by the American Music Awards, People's Choice Award and TNN Viewer's Choice Awards. In the Fall of 1993 she performed on the Country Music Association's Awards Show and caused quite a stir.

"My Lord, that child's dress was cut clear to *here*!" said one country fan, pointing to her navel. "She don't mind showing what she's got, but then that's Reba. She'll always do something to get people talking."

This country fan was referring to the black dress worn by Reba while she sang a duet, "Does He Love You," with her background singer Gail Davis. It was a powerful performance and the duo received a standing ovation. Later in the telecast, Reba took her seat in the audience beside husband Narvel Blackstock dressed in a more modest outfit.

The plane crash was clearly behind her, but just as clearly it had made a major impact on her life. Soon after the crash she had to find songs for a new album, and the songs reflected her emotions. The album, *For My Broken Heart*, begins with the title cut, a big ballad about a marriage breaking up. But the message is clear: life still goes on no matter what individual problems emerge. The world will continue to turn in spite of our personal tragedies.

"Is There Life Out There" is the story of a woman who is living an unfulfilled life; her career and dreams are stifled because of her home and family. In the video that accompanies this song, Reba plays a woman who finishes college despite the interruptions and distractions of family life at home. "Bobby" is about the sensitive subject of euthanasia. In the song a man is sentenced to prison because he pulled the life-support system plug on his wife; this causes his son to hate him. But as the song progresses the son grows to understand his dad's dilemma and reason for doing what he did, and a reconciliation is held in prison. "He's in Dallas" is a song about two young people who fall in love and move to Dallas, where the marriage ends because he's chasing his dreams while she is left to return to her mama.

In "All Dressed Up (With Nowhere to Go)" an old lady in a nursing home gets dressed up for visitors but nobody comes. It is a chilling look at old age and nursing homes in America, and about the loneliness and pain each of us may face some day. "The Night the Lights Went Out in Georgia" is the Vicki Lawrence hit written by Bobby Russell that tells the story of a young wife gone astray. Her husband finds out and sets out to kill the guy who led her astray, but discovers the guy is already dead. The husband is innocent of the crime but is hanged; then it is revealed the singer —the husband's little sister—did the shooting. "Buying Her Roses" is about a marriage that is ending so the husband courts another woman.

The World War II generation became known as the "Silent Majority" during the late 1960s and early 1970s. The model for men was the "strong, silent type," personified by the cowboy heroes, especially John Wayne, who let their actions speak for them. But the following generation wanted feelings expressed, vocal affirmation of their thoughts and feelings, sensitivity in everyday life. The song "The Greatest Man I Never Knew" addresses this generation gap. The song is ostensibly about a father who died and the child who realizes she loved and admired him—but never really knew him because he never shared his inner feelings with her. It is an admonition to the older generation as well as the current one.

Reba returns to the theme of pursuing a career at the expense of a family and home life in "I Wouldn't Go That Far." At the beginning of the song she resists pre-marital sex for marriage, then wants him to wait longer while she chases her dreams. Later in her life she sees him with his wife and family and because they've both achieved what they wanted—him a home and family and her a career—they are both happy.

In "If I Had Only Known" Reba directly addresses the tragedy of the plane crash. This song tells of the regrets at not appreciating life in the here and now because someone she loves dies suddenly. It closes the album but does not close this chapter in Reba's life. In an interview with journalist Chet Flippo a few months after her band members had died, she said, "I'll tell you what that accident taught me more than anything else. You have to get your ducks in a row. You may think you're walking on the top rail, but you can fall off any minute. I mean, you'd better get your life straight. You know that old saying? 'Man makes plans, and God laughs!'" Reba added that "Honest to God, before that crash, I thought we were invincible. Now, though, you know you're so touchable, so vulnerable."

Reba and Narvel had bought another plane identical to the one that crashed soon after the accident. They had looked at a number of planes but decided on that one although Reba admitted "At first, just saying that name reminded me every time."

Increasingly, what pulled her life together—and pulled her through hard, difficult times—was her new family. Narvel is not just her husband and manager, he is a rock she can lean on. And her son, Shelby, is the emotional core of her life. The first three years of Shelby's life saw Reba go through some immense changes.

At the beginning of 1990, Reba was very pregnant and very excited. "I'm so excited I can hardly stand it," she told a reporter for a woman's magazine. "We're re-doing the house, and I go into the nursery and tell the baby, 'Here's your room.' I talk to the baby a lot. The baby is my buddy. I saw an ultrasound picture of it, and I think that was the first time I really knew I was pregnant. Before that, I thought I was just sick a lot. But when I finally saw the picture, I said, 'Why, you little rascal! There you are!'"

She was feeling in a family way in more ways than one. "I'd love to have four or five kids, I really would," she exclaimed. "But we have to plan in this business, especially since I have about forty people on the payroll. When this baby is one year and three months old, I wanna get pregnant again. The kids will all have the same birthday month—March—but the first four months of the year are not as good for touring as July through November are."

She was obviously happily married, telling the reporter, "Wow! Do we get along good! Yep, it's a great marriage.

"It's real weird but I probably would have never picked Narvel as my husband," she said, noting that she had known him for ten years, meeting him when he came to work for her as her steel-guitar player. "And he probably wouldn't have picked me. But it's just one of those things."

Motherhood was tickling her pink. "This is the news I've been waiting thirty-four years to hear—that I'm having a baby," she told the reporter. "Before, I wasn't with the right partner for children. I had to wait for the right daddy. I wanted a man who's loving and understanding and giving. Narvel is—and he's a very good daddy. I admire the way he handles situations. You don't want your children to have a daddy who is impersonal and cold and crude and rude and abusive."

When the reporter asked about her first husband, Reba's eyes flashed. "That's the one thing I don't want to talk about—Charlie Battles," she said emphatically. "He's history." Testily, she continued. "I don't have any association with that marriage—not with Charlie and not with his two sons from a previous marriage. When something's over for me, it's over. I never see him. I never write, I never call, I never send Christmas cards. Nothing. I moved out, I left. I came to Nashville."

On February 23, 1990 in Nashville, it was cloudy with a chilly wind, and the forecast called for a cold front. At West Side Hospital, Reba was in labor in the early morning hours. Then, at 5:04 A.M., little Shelby Stephen McEntire Blackstock entered the world.

Later, Reba said, "Once you go through childbirth, and it's so dramatic, because it's a life-and-death situation, everything else is very minor."

After she got the baby home she said, "All the surprises, everything about motherhood, is the greatest thing in the world. It's fun to do, but it's a chore. It's very hard. All the time, twenty-four hours a day, you're responsible for this child. But I love doin' it."

Shelby did not want for gifts when he got home, and Reba joked that she could open a museum of baby gifts. She got "tons" of hand-crocheted items from fans; a stick horse and blanket came from Wynonna and Naomi Judd; Barbara Mandrell's son, Nathan, sent a wooden airplane; Minnie Pearl gave an outfit; a blue teddy bear came from Hank Williams, Jr. From Reba's family, Shelby got cowboy boots from Grandma and Grandpa McEntire and a cowboy hat from Uncle Pake and Aunt Kate. As for Reba, she said, "Oh, I'm tellin' you, we're gonna get him a horse next year!"

In May, 1990, Reba had hit the road touring again, often taking Shelby along or flying back after a concert to be with him. But being a mother now meant her career wasn't the all-important, all-encompassing thing in her life. "The things I used to think were important, they can wait now," said Reba. "Wherever I go, he goes with me. We just troop along."

And she reflected back on her own childhood, traveling to rodeos with her parents. "Whenever Mom and Daddy traveled to rodeo contests, they took us kids along in their ol' green Ford," she reminisced. "We adapted very well. That's the one reason I'm not worried about taking my baby on the concert circuit. It doesn't matter if you're at home or on the road, just as long as you're together. When I'm traveling with my baby during the summer months, it'll be like those times when I traveled with my daddy. That was our summer vacation and we had a blast!"

Three years later she is still enthused about her marriage and family life, although she admits there's been a lot of changes. The main reason is Shelby. "He's made me much more patient," said Reba. "He's made me less selfish. I think that's the biggest change. Before I became a mother, it was all Reba, Reba, Reba. What can Reba do now? And what can Reba do for Reba as an entertainer? And what can Reba do for Reba's career? Now I think of my family. It really does open your eyes to have kids. Besides, you have no more time for yourself."

But the plane crash has also had a major effect on her. "Everything changed," said Reba. "I married a man I totally love, love to be with, respect, admire, trust. Then I had Shelby with him. With Shelby it was total happiness and bliss; he gave me something in my life that I had never been given before. When the tragedy happened, I felt like saying, 'Screw this, I don't ever want to love anybody else again; I don't ever want to get close to anybody.'

"On the other hand," she continued, "that's not the lesson to learn from this. It's love every minute you can, live life to the fullest, each minute as if it is your last. Learn from it—get your ducks in a row, get right with God. Where do you go, what do you believe in , what do you feel in your heart is the right thing to do? I grew immensely. I went within myself; I was a pretty outward person, and I'm more of an inward person now. I listen more; I'm quieter."

Reba had examined her life and her faith and gone deep within herself in the months after the crash. "I was never mad at God," she said. "I knew that it happened for a reason, so I trusted Him; I know He knows best. That brought Narvel and me real close together because he leaned on me. I leaned on him; we were inseparable during the ordeal. It made me realize that my time can be any minute, Narvel's time can be any minute, so could Shelby's, my mom, dad, brother and sisters."

In some ways, Reba's personal life improved after the tragedy. She committed herself to her marriage and noted, "You've got to work at marriage. I don't care if you marry the person of your all-time dreams and you're madly in love—it's work. It's a lot of work. These little ole kids that bebop into a marriage and think they want a roommate, somebody to pal around with, they're in for the shock of the century! And there are a lot of days I could just say, 'Forget it,' but I boo-booed on the first; I don't want to boo-boo again."

Reba admits that "I'm real bad to sulk up and brood, so I know immediately when that happens, it's confrontation time. It needs to be in our bedroom quiet at night, when nobody else is around—then we have it out." She reflects, "That's probably what caused my first divorce—I didn't talk about it."

The focus of her life is now her son. "Shelby is the first thing I think of in the morning," she says. When she wakes up in the morning, "I just want to go see Shelby. I get him out of his bed and put him in bed with me and Narvel, and we just play and have a good time. When I'm at work, that's who I want to go home to, 'cause Narvel is here at work and I get to see him every day. I want to go home and see Shelby—then I can't wait till Narvel gets home. It's just a real good life."

2

At the beginning of 1990 Reba's first movie, a horror-movie parody, "Tremors," was just out. In it she played the wife of a survivalist couple with "Family Ties" star Michael Gross.

She admitted that acting was harder than she thought it was. "I didn't have an audience," she said. "I had a camera to look into, and it wasn't as interesting and exciting to me as live television."

In the movie she has lines like "Hand me that forty-aught seventy-two bore Mega repeater with the dual cartridges." But it was fun, and that's why she had agreed to the movie in the first place.

When her agent had originally called her about the script, she had said, "I don't like horror pitchers [sic]. I don't like monster flicks." But he insisted she read so she did, then called him back. "This is hilarious," she said. "I want to read for it."

On the set, Reba got to explore the character herself. "They didn't give me any coaching whatsoever," she said. "They let me wing it completely. I'd go to 'em and I'd say, 'How do you see this part?' And they'd say, 'How do you see it?' I would tell them and they'd say 'Fine.'

"In all honesty, I played Reba McEntire," she said. "Narvel's my best friend; Heather and Burt [the characters in "Tremors"] were best friends and good buddies, and whenever we're together, that's the way Narvel and I do in the music business and our family life." The filming in the desert was hot and tough, but she only complained about one thing: there wasn't a port-a-potty. A call to her agent solved that.

In the fall of 1991, after the plane crash, she received an offer for her next movie, the role of Burgundy, a madame in Kenny Rogers' made-for-TV movie "The Luck of the Draw: The Gambler Returns" on NBC. Acting was a new challenge for her, but one she clearly enjoyed meeting.

"I chose to get into acting," she said. "Just to see what it was like, to try it, to see if I could do it; to see if I would be accepted in the movie industry. I cheated because I went on my name; you can always get in a little bit easier if you have a name already." But after she got the part, she wondered "how many aspiring young actresses read for this part, dying to get it." From this point, said Reba, "I took it more seriously then. I really started working hard because I don't want to take anything away from anybody who deserves it more than I do. And then it became a big deal for me for it to work, for me to do good."

In the movie *North* Reba worked with director Rob Reiner. In the movie she plays a character, Ma Texas, who is married to the character played by Dan Aykroyd. According to Reba, "The movie's about a kid who divorces his parents and has from July 4 to Labor Day to find a new set of parents. We're the first set he tries out."

The acting has given Reba a new ambition. "I want to win an Oscar," she states flatly.

Still, the emphasis is on her singing career. In 1992 her album *It's Your Call* had been released. On this album there was a duet with Vince Gill, "The Heart Won't Lie," as well as "Take It Back" and "It's Your Call." The theme of marriages in trouble and breaking up was again prevalent with "It's Your Call" about a man cheating on his wife and "Straight From You" where the wife demands to know the truth about some gossip she's heard about her husband. Infidelity is also dealt with in "Take It Back" but in a gutsy, confrontational way; clearly the woman is taking charge of this situation.

"He Wants to Get Married" is about finding a good man who wants to marry and settle down and the woman is glad she's found him. In "One Last Good Hand" love is once more affirmed, finding a dream man who can share dreams.

In "For Herself" a woman takes charge of her life and asserts her independence by leaving her husband; in "Will He Ever Go" the man has gone, but the memory lingers on, and the woman can't seem to get back on track. The album concludes with "Lighter Shade of Blue," a song that on the surface is about someone who's left but still remembered. But on another level, this song could be about the plane tragedy where the band members will never come back and the singer admits she will always be blue—but at least it is a shade lighter as time goes by.

3

In 1901—when Reba's Grandma McEntire was born—there were forty-five states in the Union, and women could not vote in forty of them. In three-fourths of the states, women were prohibited from owning property in their own name. In a third of the states, a woman had no legal right to her own earnings, and only a fifth of the states gave a woman equal rights with her husband in the guardianship of their children. When someone in the family died, women wore black clothes and "mourning veils" for a year and all amusements were taboo.

Reba's Grandma McEntire had a tough life; it was not until after World War II that electricity was widespread in rural southeastern Oklahoma. That meant that cooking, ironing, and canning all had to be done over a hot stove, even in the summer when the temperature stayed in the 90s and there was no air conditioning. Today Reba will use more electricity in one concert show than her grandmother did during her entire life.

Reba is never happier than when she has a new album and another tour because this provides the impetus for her to do what she loves doing more than anything else in the world: getting up in front of an audience and singing. It's what she was put on this earth to do and there's no greater feeling than doing what it is you're called to do, being who you are, living the life you've always wanted to live and watching your dreams come true.

She is excited about being a wife, a mother, a recording artist, and an entertainer. And there are still more things to do, more places to be, more people to sing to. "If I'm bored, my audiences are gonna be bored," she says. "And if I know that I can do it better, we've gotta find somethin' better. No, when you get satisfied and you're not hungry anymore, that's for me a good signal for Reba to stay home and raise children and buy a laundromat!"

In spite of her love for her family and all the new priorities she has set in her own life, the hunger is still there to perform, to reach out to audiences, to be a star bigger and brighter than all the other stars combined. That pursuit of stardom is the one constant in her life. In 1987, when she got her divorce, she says that "the Scripture I was reading at that time really gave me a lot of strength. It said, 'The person who is behind the mule plow in the field and looks back is the fool'...At the time I was going through the divorce, I did nothing but plow on. It worked, I changed my life, moving from Oklahoma to Tennessee, just staying busy and trying to think up bigger and better things to do in my career."

Reba has built a huge career as an artist, as well as a business empire with her company, Starstruck. This company, located near the Tennessee State Fairgrounds, several miles from Music Row in a converted warehouse, keeps her whole career under one roof: management, booking, publicity, the fan club, even her busses. Still, she is not satisfied. "When I think about what I've accomplished, it's satisfying," she says. "But then someone like Garth Brooks or Billy Ray Cyrus comes along and knocks my accomplishments to the side of the road." It's true that the "new country" artists have come along and displaced a number of the older stars, but Reba continues to be the woman who dominates country music.

Still, it ain't easy being a woman in country music and Reba reminds everyone of this. "Women have to work hard and prove themselves—she's a 'bitch,' where a man is 'tough,'" she relates. "They have to get around that, work harder and basically keep their mouth shut and prove themselves, which is not fair, but that's the bottom line, the ink in bold letters. That's what I have learned. I've done very well, but I didn't cram myself down anybody's throat, I didn't say, 'Because I'm a woman, you have to give me this.' I just worked twice as hard and I don't demand anything."

She has her six-bedroom house on an 80-acre ranch that's filled with horses named after her songs. She left her ranch in Oklahoma in June 1987, but the ranch life was too deeply embedded in her to abandon it totally. In Thanksgiving that year she and Narvel and his three children by a previous marriage visited Reba's parents in Oklahoma. And one of Narvel's kids discovered the joys of horses and ranching so Reba and Narvel bought him a horse.

At Christmas 1987 Reba got a big surprise when Narvel presented her with a horse, Little Bit. "I'd never really had a horse of my own," she said. "And I'd never had a saddle of my own." She got the saddle from her office staff that same Christmas.

But her singing is what means most to Reba, so she is always looking for new songs to sing. "Looking for the monster song is all I've ever done since I got control over my music," she states. "I want something that's going to give me chills. If something is rock'n'roll, bluegrass, whatever, it doesn't matter: Whatever I sing is going to come out country. The idea is to sing something that everyone can relate to."

As another year drew to a close she reflected, "No matter what you achieve in life, you're always wondering, 'Is there something I should be doing? Is there something I'm missing?' You may have all the money in the world and the fame and the glory, but the smallest, simplest things will bring you more pleasure than that."

Singing is fame and fortune, the Big Career for Reba, but it's also a simple pleasure. "I've quit trying to analyze and now I just sing," she says about her songs and their impact on audiences. Most of her dreams have come true and others will soon. She lives a good life and she knows it and feels blessed. There are endless demands that must be satisfied to keep a career like Reba's going. But she loves it and thrives on it.

As Reba herself says, "It's hard work, for sure, but it's the best I've found."

231

ALBUMS

Reba McEntire

Mercury SRM-1-5002
Producer: Jerry Kennedy

Side 1

"Glad I Waited Just for You"
"One to One"
"Angel in Your Arms"
"I Don't Want to Be a One Night Stand"*
"I've Waited All My Life for You"
"I Was Glad to Give My Everything to You"

Side 2

"Take Your Love Away"
"(There's Nothing Like the Love) Between a Woman and a Man"

*Produced by Glenn Keener

"Why Can't He Be You"
"Invitation to the Blues"
"Right Time of the Night"

Out of a Dream

Mercury SRM 1-5017
Producer: Jerry Kennedy

Side 1

"(I Still Long to Hold You) Now and Then"
"Daddy"
"Last Night, Ev'ry Night"
"Make Me Feel Like a Woman Wants to Feel"
"That Makes Two of Us"

Side 2

"Sweet Dreams"
"I'm a Woman"
"Rain Fallin' "
"Runaway Heart"
"It's Gotta Be Love"

Feel the Fire

Mercury SRM-1-5029
Producer: Jerry Kennedy

Side 1

"(You Lift Me) Up to Heaven"
"Tears on My Pillow"
"I Don't Think Love Ought to Be That Way"
"Long Distance Lover"
"If I Had My Way"

Side 2

"I Can See Forever in Your Eyes"
"A Poor Man's Roses (Or a Rich Man's Gold)"
"My Turn"

"Look at the One (Who's Been Lookin' at You)"
"Suddenly There's a Valley"

Heart to Heart

Mercury SRM-1-6003
Producer: Jerry Kennedy

Side 1
"Indelibly Blue"
"Ease the Fever"
"There Ain't No Love"
"How Does It Feel to Be Free"
"Only You (And You Alone)"

Side 2
"Today All Over Again"
"Gonna Love You (Till the Cows Come Home)"
"Who?"
"Small Two-Bedroom Starter"
"Love by Love"

Unlimited

Polygram SRM-1-4047
Producer: Jerry Kennedy

Side 1
"I'd Say You"
"Everything I'll Ever Own"
"What Do You Know About Heartache"
"Out of the Blue"
"Over, Under, and Around"

Side 2
"I'm Not That Lonely Yet"
"Whoever's Watchin'"
"Old Man River (I've Come to Talk Again)"

"You're the First Time I've Thought About Leaving"
"Can't Even Get the Blues"

Behind the Scene

Polygram 422-812 781-1 M-1
Producer: Jerry Kennedy

Side 1

"Love Isn't Love (Till You Give It Away)"
"Is It Really Love"
"Reasons"
"Nickel Dreams"
"One Good Reason"

Side 2

"You Really Better Love Me After This"
"There Ain't No Future in This"
"Why Do We Want (What We Know We Can't Have)"
"I Sacrificed More Than You'll Ever Lose"
"Pins and Needles"

Just a Little Love

MCA 5475
Producer: Norro Wilson

Side 1

"Just a Little Love"
"Poison Sugar"
"I'm Gettin' Over You"
"You Are Always There for Me"
"Every Second Someone Breaks a Heart"

Side 2

"Tell Me What's So Good About Goodbye"
"He Broke Your Mem'ry Last Night"
"If Only"

"Congratulations"
"Silver Eagle"

My Kind of Country

MCA 5516
Producer: Harold Shedd

Side 1

"How Blue"
"That's What He Said"
"I Want to Hear It From You"
"It's Not Over (If I'm Not Over You)"
"Somebody Should Leave"

Side 2

"Everything But My Heart"
"Don't You Believe Him"
"Before I Met You"
"He's Only Everything"
"You've Got Me (Right Where You Want Me)"

Have I Got a Deal for You

MCA 5585
Producers: Jimmy Bowen and Reba McEntire

Side 1

"I'm in Love All Over"
"She's Single Again"
"The Great Divide"
"Have I Got a Deal for You"
"Red Roses (Won't Work Now)"

Side 2

"Only in My Mind"
"She's the One Loving You Now"
"Whose Heartache Is This Anyway?"

"I Don't Need Nothin' You Ain't Got"
"Don't Forget Your Way Home"

Whoever's in New England

MCA 5691
Producers: Jimmy Bowen and Reba McEntire

Side 1
"Can't Stop Now"
"You Can Take the Wings off Me"
"Whoever's in New England"
"I'll Believe It When I Feel It"
"I've Seen Better Days"

Side 2
"Little Rock"
"If You Only Knew"
"One Thin Dime"
"Don't Touch Me There"
"Don't Make That Same Mistake Again"

What Am I Gonna Do About You

MCA 5807
Producers: Jimmy Bowen and Reba McEntire

Side 1
"Why Not Tonight"
"What Am I Gonna Do About You"
"Lookin' for a New Love Story"
"Take Me Back"
"My Mind Is on You"

Side 2
"Let the Music Lift You"
"I Heard Her Cryin'"
"No Such Thing"

"One Promise Too Late"
"Till It Snows in Mexico"

Greatest Hits

MCA 5979

Side 1
"Just a Little Love"
"He Broke Your Mem'ry Last Night"
"How Blue"
"Somebody Should Leave"
"Have I Got a Deal for You"

Side 2
"Only in My Mind"
"Whoever's in New England"
"Little Rock"
"What Am I Gonna Do About You"
"One Promise Too Late"

Reba Nell McEntire

Polygram 822 455-1 M-1
Producer: Jerry Kennedy

Side 1
"I've Never Stopped Dreaming of You"
"Hold On"
"I Know I'll Have a Better Day Tomorrow"
"Don't Say Good Night, Say Good Morning"
"Muddy Mississippi"

Side 2
"It's Another Silent Night"
"Empty Arms"
"Love Is Never Easy"
"Waitin' for the Sun to Shine"
"Good Friends"

The Last One to Know

MCA 42030
Producers: Jimmy Bowen and Reba McEntire

Side 1

"The Last One to Know"
"The Girl Who Has Everything"
"Just Across the Rio Grande"
"I Don't Want to Mention Any Names"
"Someone Else"

Side 2

"What You Gonna Do About Me"
"I Don't Want to Be Alone"
"The Stairs"
"Love Will Find Its Way to You"
"I've Still Got the Love We Made"

Christmas

MCA 42031
Producers: Jimmy Bowen and Reba McEntire

Side 1

"Away in a Manger"
"On This Day"
"O Holy Night"
"The Christmas Guest"
"Silent Night"

Side 2

"Happy Birthday Jesus (I'll Open This One for You)"
"White Christmas"
"I'll Be Home for Christmas"
"A Christmas Letter"
"The Christmas Song (Chestnuts Roasting on an Open Fire)"

Reba

MCA 42134
Producers: Jimmy Bowen and Reba McEntire

Side 1

"So, So, So Long"
"Sunday Kind of Love"
"New Fool at an Old Game"
"You're the One I Dream About"
"Silly Me"

Side 2

"Respect"
"Do Right by Me"
"I Know How He Feels"
"Wish I Were Only Lonely"
"Everytime You Touch Her"

Sweet Sixteen

MCA 6294
Producers: Jimmy Bowen and Reba McEntire

Side 1

"Cathy's Clown"
"'Til Love Comes Again"
"It Always Rains on Saturday"
"Am I the Only One Who Cares"
"Somebody Up There Likes Me"

Side 2

"You Must Really Love Me"
"Say the Word"
"Little Girl"
"Walk On"
"A New Love"

240

Reba Live

MCA C2-8034
Producers: Jimmy Bowen and Reba McEntire

Side 1

"So, So, So Long"
"One Promise Too Late"
"Let the Music Lift You Up"
"Little Rock"
"New Fool at an Old Game"
"Little Girl"
"Can't Stop Now"
"Sunday Kind of Love"
"I Know How He Feels"

Side 2

"Whoever's in New England"
"Cathy's Clown"
"You Must Really Love Me"
"Somebody Up There Likes Me"
"San Antonio Rose"
"Mama Tried"
"Night Life"
"Jolene"
"Sweet Dreams"
"Respect"

Rumor Has It

MCA 10016
Producer: Tony Brown and Reba McEntire

Side 1

"Climb That Mountain High"
"Rumor Has It"
"Waitin' for the Deal to Go Down"

"You Lie"
"Now You Tell Me"

Side 2

"Fancy"
"Fallin' out of Love"
"This Picture"
"You Remember Me"
"That's All She Wrote"

S I N G L E S

Reba McEntire

"The Ballad of John McEntire" Boss
"I Don't Want to Be a One Night Stand" Mercury 73788
(#88)*
"(There's Nothing Like the Love) Between a Woman and a
Man" Mercury 73879 (#86)
"Glad I Waited Just for You" Mercury 73929 (#88)
"Last Night, Ev'ry Night" Mercury 55036 (#28)
"Runaway Heart" Mercury 55058 (#36)
"Sweet Dreams" Mercury 57003 (#19)
"(I Still Long to Hold You) Now and Then" Mercury
57014 (#40)
"(You Lift Me) Up to Heaven" Mercury 57075 (#8)
"I Can See Forever in Your Eyes" Mercury 57034 (#18)
"I Don't Think Love Ought to Be That Way" Mercury
57046 (#13)
"Today All Over Again" Mercury 57054 (#5)
"Only You (And You Alone)" Mercury 57062 (#13)
"I'm Not That Lonely Yet" Mercury 76157 (#3)

*Numbers in parentheses denote a single's highest placement on the *Billboard*
Country Singles chart.

"Can't Even Get the Blues" Mercury 76180 (#1)
"You're the First Time I've Thought About Leaving"
Mercury 810338 (#1)
"Why Do We Want (What We Know We Can't Have)"
Mercury 812632 (#7)
"There Ain't No Future in This" Mercury 814629 (#12)
"Just a Little Love" MCA 52349 (#5)
"He Broke Your Mem'ry Last Night" MCA 52404 (#15)
"How Blue" MCA 52468 (#1)
"Somebody Should Leave" MCA 52527 (#1)
"Have I Got a Deal for You" MCA 52604 (#6)
"Only in My Mind" MCA 52691 (#5)
"Whoever's in New England" MCA 52767 (#1)
"Little Rock" MCA 52848 (#1)
"What Am I Gonna Do About You" MCA 52922 (#1)
"Let the Music Lift You [Up]" MCA 52990 (#4)
"One Promise Too Late" MCA 53092 (#1)
"The Last One to Know" MCA 53159 (#1)
"Love Will Find Its Way to You" MCA 53244 (#1)
"Sunday Kind of Love" MCA 53315 (#5)
"I Know How He Feels" MCA 53402 (#1)
"New Fool at an Old Game" MCA 53473 (#1)

Jacky Ward and Reba McEntire

"Three Sheets in the Wind" b/w "I'd Really Love to See
You Tonight" Mercury 55026 (#20)
"That Makes Two of Us" Mercury 55054 (#26)

BIBLIOGRAPHY

AND SOURCES

The files at the Country Music Foundation were my first and perhaps most valuable source as I began this book. I also used files from the Cowboy and Rodeo Hall of Fame in Oklahoma City, the files from the Rodeo Hall of Fame in Colorado Springs, and some files from the Historical Society in McAlester, Oklahoma. I also visited the Court Houses in McAlester and Atoka, Oklahoma, and Nashville and Lebanon, Tennessee, for records.

In researching rodeos, the book *Rodeo: An Anthropologist Looks at the Wild and the Tame* by Elizabeth Atwood Lawrence was especially helpful; also used were *Let 'er Buck!: The Rodeo* by Barbara Berry, *American Rodeo: From Buffalo Bill to Big Business* by Kristine Fredriksson, *They Ride the Rodeo: The Men and Women of the American Amateur Rodeo Circuit* by Joe Englander, and *Cowboy Culture: A Saga of Five Centuries* by David Dary.

For the history of Stringtown, the book *Tales of Atoka County Heritage*, published by The Atoka County Historical Society, provided most of the factual background. For a general history of Oklahoma, I used *Oklahoma: A History of Five Centuries* by Arrell Morgan Gibson.

In *The Illustrated History of Country Music*, edited by Patrick Carr, two chapters: "Music From the Lone Star State" by Doug Green and Bob Pinson, and "The Singing Cowboys" by J. R. Young were extremely helpful in understanding western music and the singing cowboys. Also particularly helpful was the chapter on Gene Autry by Doug Green in *Stars of Country Music*, edited by Bill Malone and Judith McCullough.

Joel Whitburn's books on country music charts from *Billboard* was an invaluable source when checking on Reba's (and everybody else's) recordings.

The essay "From Hero to Celebrity" by Daniel Boorstin in his book *Hidden History* provided some key ideas, and a section in *The Path to Power*, the excellent biography of Lyndon Johnson by Robert Caro, was helpful in understanding rural life in Oklahoma before electricity.

In addition to traditional sources, I read some books that were especially enlightening and inspirational for this work. *Passages* by Gail Sheehy is an excellent book for understanding changes men and women go through in their lives; *With Malice Toward None* by Stephen Oates, the excellent biography of Abraham Lincoln, gave me the idea of using short sections as a stylistic device; and the novels of Louis L'Amour got me in the spirit of the West whenever I needed it. Michael Martin Murphey's album *Cowboy Songs* kept me company through many hours of editing.

I talked with and interviewed a number of people in researching this book, most of whom are mentioned in the Acknowledgments, though I would especially like to thank Clark Rhyne, Charlie Battles, and Ray Williams.

Finally, I have used my experiences covering country music since 1973 and research done for a course I teach, "History of the Recording Industry," for several passages in this book. These include some historical background as well as observations about how country music and Nashville function "behind the scenes."